CSET®

Mathematics Practice Questions

Mometrix

TEST PREPARATION

DEAR FUTURE EXAM SUCCESS STORY

First of all, **THANK YOU** for purchasing Mometrix study materials!

Second, congratulations! You are one of the few determined test-takers who are committed to doing whatever it takes to excel on your exam. **You have come to the right place.** We developed these practice tests with one goal in mind: to deliver you the best possible approximation of the questions you will see on test day.

Standardized testing is one of the biggest obstacles on your road to success, which only increases the importance of doing well in the high-pressure, high-stakes environment of test day. Your results on this test could have a significant impact on your future, and these practice tests will give you the repetitions you need to build your familiarity and confidence with the test content and format to help you achieve your full potential on test day.

Your success is our success

We would love to hear from you! If you would like to share the story of your exam success or if you have any questions or comments in regard to our products, please contact us at **800-673-8175** or **support@mometrix.com**.

Thanks again for your business and we wish you continued success!

Sincerely,
The Mometrix Test Preparation Team

Table of Contents

Practice Test #1

1. Aaron goes on a run every morning down the straight country road that he lives on. The graph below shows Aaron's distance from home at times throughout his morning run. Which of the following statements is (are) true?

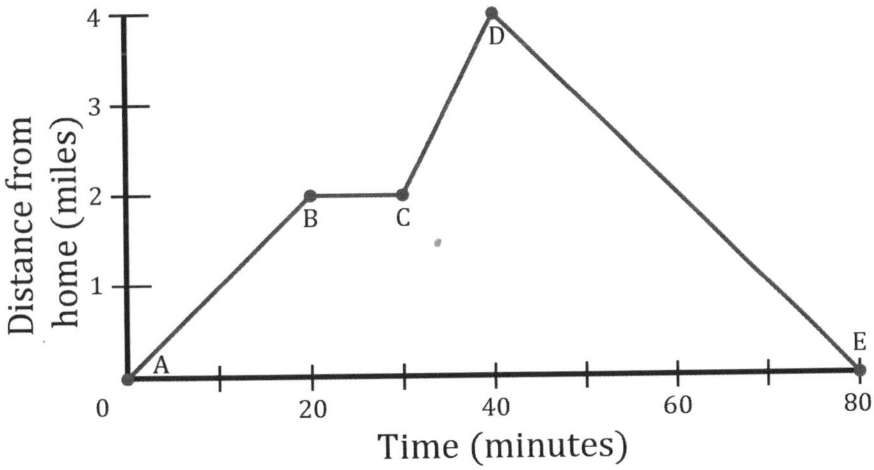

I. Aaron's average running speed was 6 mph.
II. Aaron's running speed from A to B was the same as from D to E.
III. Aaron ran a total distance of four miles.

a. I only
b. II only
c. I and II
d. I, II, and III

2. To test the accuracy and precision of two scales, a student repeatedly measured the mass of a 25g standard and recorded these results.

	Trial 1	Trial 2	Trial 3	Trial 4
Scale 1	24.65 g	24.67 g	24.66 g	24.65 g
Scale 2	24.95 g	25.07 g	24.98 g	25.03 g

Which of these conclusions about the scales is true?

a. Scale 1 has an average percent error of 1.37%, and Scale 2 has an average percent error of 0.23%. Scale 2 is more accurate and precise than Scale 1.
b. Scale 1 has an average percent error of 1.37%, and Scale 2 has an average percent error of 0.23%. Scale 2 is more accurate than Scale 1; however, Scale 1 is more precise.
c. Scale 1 has an average percent error of 1.37%, and Scale 2 has an average percent error of 0.17%. Scale 2 is more accurate and precise than Scale 1.
d. Scale 1 has an average percent error of 1.37%, and Scale 2 has an average percent error of 0.17%. Scale 2 is more accurate than Scale 1; however, Scale 1 is more precise.

3. Krystal purchased a pair of sunglasses for $19.99 and a scarf for $27.50. She paid with a $50.00 bill. How much change did she receive?

a. $47.49
b. $17.49
c. $3.61
d. $2.99
e. $2.51

4. Which of these graphs is representative of the data set shown below?

Stem	Leaf
1	2 6 6 8 9
2	2 3 6
3	0 1 4 4 5 7
4	2 2 2 4 5 9

KEY

$2|123 = 21, 22, 23$

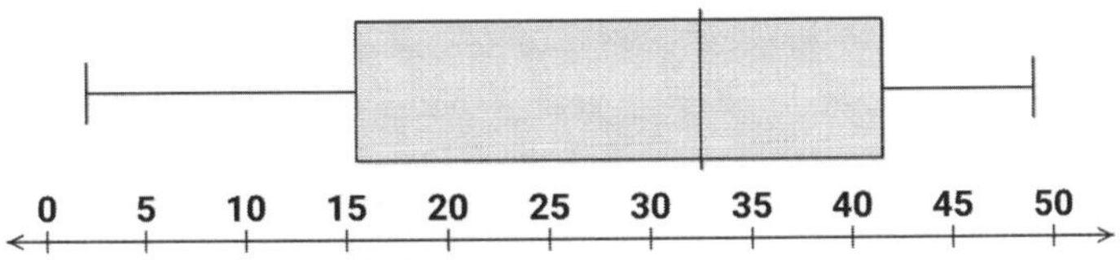

a.

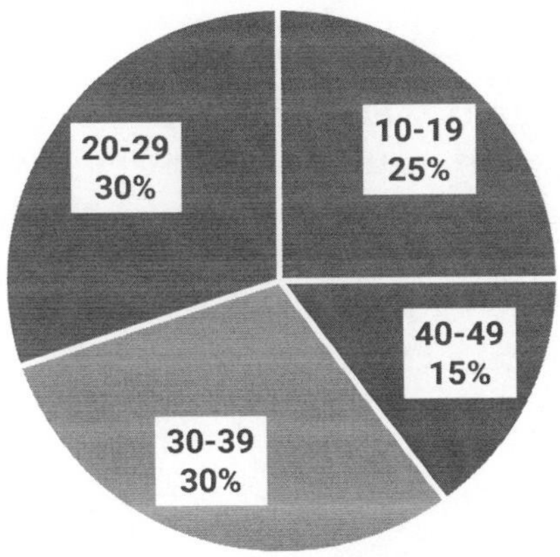

b.

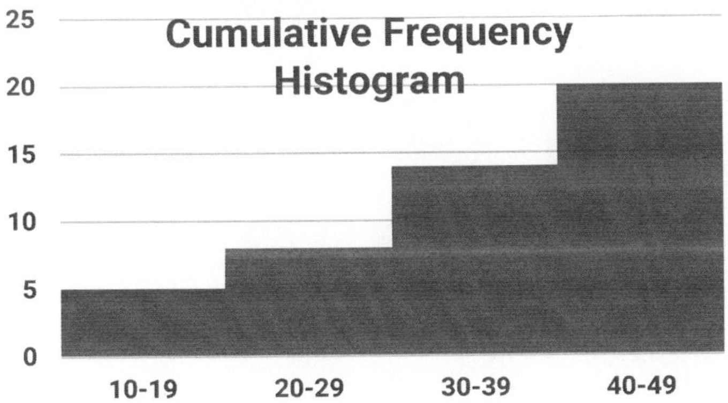

c.

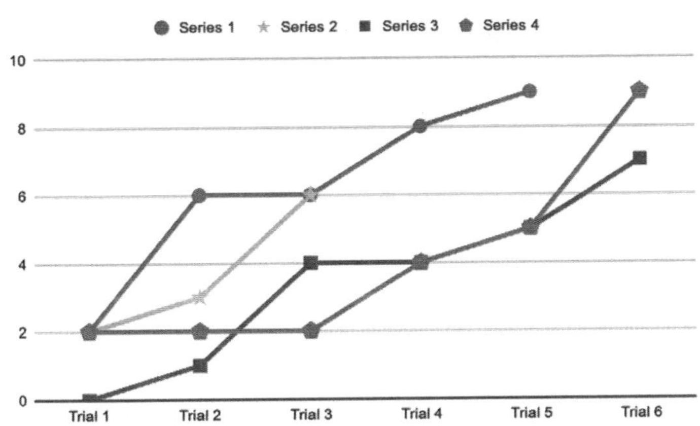

d.

5. Jan creates a mosaic with tiles in the shape of congruent isosceles triangles, as seen below. What is the value of x in the figure?

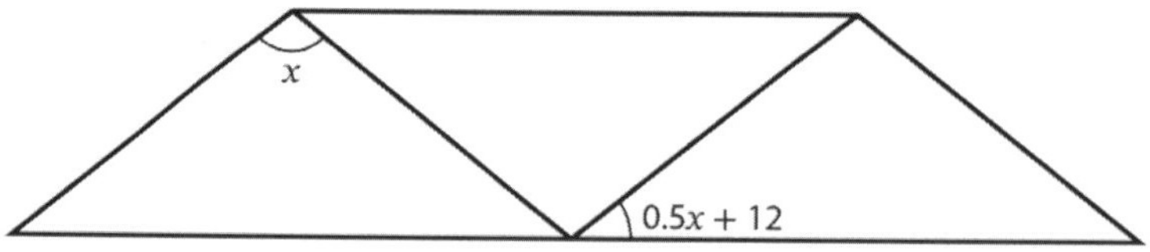

a. $x = 56$
b. $x = 78$
c. $x = 89.5$
d. The value of x cannot be determined from the information given.

6. A round table has six chairs, labeled H–M. If the chairs were arranged in a straight line in the same order that they have around the table, chair H would be on one end and chair K on the other. Chair J would be between chairs H and I, chair L would be between chairs I and M, and chair M would be between chairs L and K. Which of the statements is/are necessarily true based solely on the information provided?

I. The distance between chairs H and L is greater than the distance between chairs I and M.
II. Chair I is between chairs J and L.
III. The distance between chairs M and K is less than the distance between chairs H and L.

a. I, II, and III
b. I and III
c. II only
d. None of these is necessarily true

7. Complete the analogy: $y = \frac{1}{\sqrt{x}}$ is to $x = y^{-2}$ as ...

a. $y = 2x$ is to $x = y^2$.
b. $y = e^x$ is to $x = \frac{1}{e^y}$, where $y > 0$.
c. $y = \frac{1}{x^2}$ is to $x = y^2$, where $x, y \neq 0$.
d. $y = \cos x$ is to $x = \cos^{-1} y$.

8. If 1 inch on a map represents 10 feet and 1 yard is equal to 3 feet, how many yards apart are two points if the distance between the points on the map is 24 inches?

a. 240 yards
b. 80 yards
c. 24 yards
d. 12 yards

9. How many different 6-character passwords exist that follow these rules:

I. The first two characters are unique letters
II. The last four characters are unique numbers
III. The code ends with an odd number

a. 3,276,000
b. 1,638,000
c. 526,300
d. 108,000

10. Simplify: $\frac{2-5i}{3+2i}$

a. $-\frac{4}{13}+\frac{11}{13}i$
b. $\frac{15}{13}$
c. $-\frac{4}{13}-\frac{19}{13}i$
d. $\frac{16}{13}-\frac{19}{13}i$

11. Which of the following statements is (are) true when $f(x)=\frac{x^2-x-2}{x^3-7x+6}$?

I. The graph $f(x)$ has vertical asymptotes at $x=-3$, $x=1$, and $x=2$.
II. The x- and y-intercepts of the graph of $f(x)$ are both $-\frac{1}{3}$.

a. I only
b. II only
c. I and II
d. Neither statement is true.

12. The cost, in dollars, of shipping x computers to California for sale is $3,000+100x$. The amount received when selling these computers is $400x$ dollars. What is the least number of computers that must be shipped and sold so that the amount received is at least equal to the shipping cost?

a. 10 computers
b. 15 computers
c. 20 computers
d. 25 computers
e. 30 computers

Refer to the following for questions 13–14:

Each day for 100 days, a student tossed a single misshapen coin three times in succession and recorded the number of times the coin landed on heads. The results of his experiment are shown below.

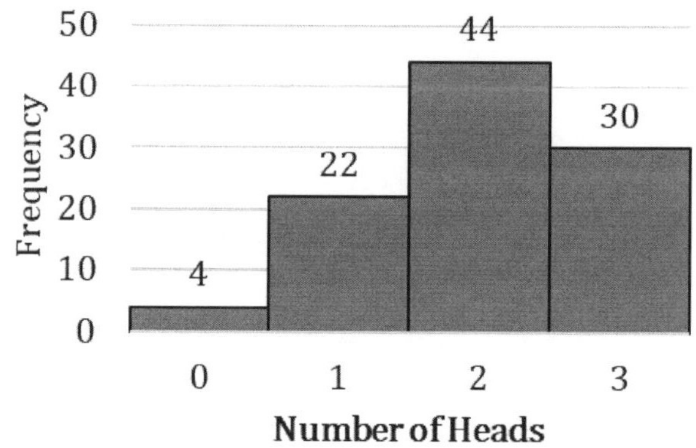

13. Given these experimental data, which of these approximates $P(\text{heads})$ for a single flip of this coin?

a. 0.22
b. 0.5
c. 0.66
d. 0.74

14. Which of these shows the graphs of the probability distributions from 10 flips of this misshapen coin and 10 flips of a fair coin?

Fair Coin   Misshapen Coin

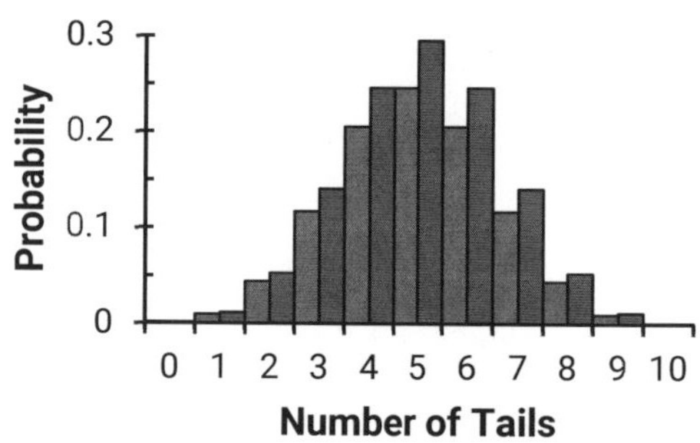

a.

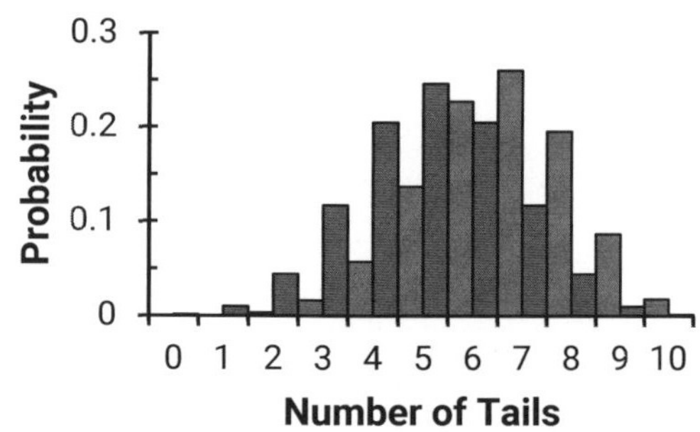

c.

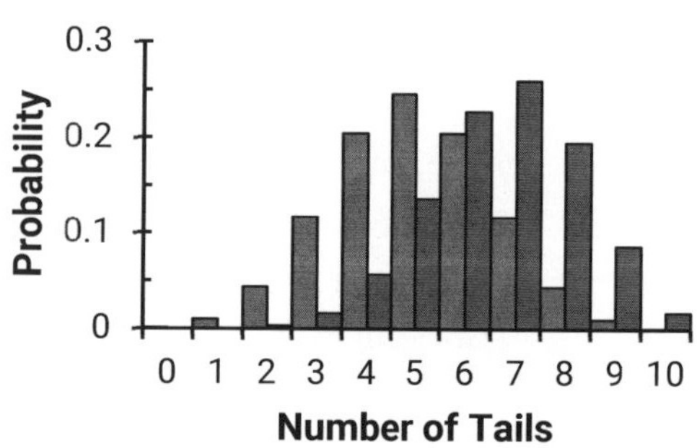

b.

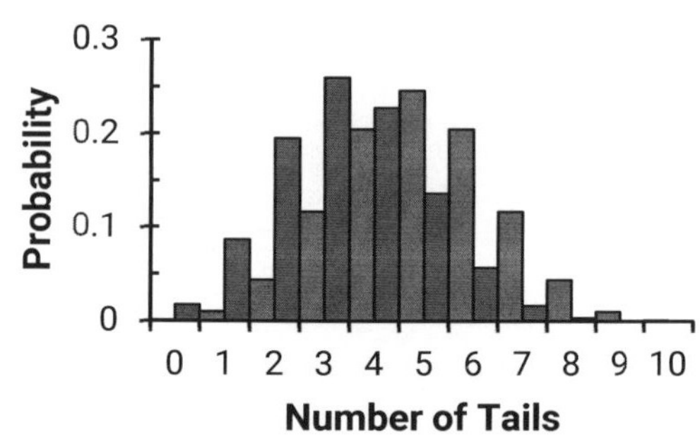

d.

15. Which of these is the least biased sampling technique?

a. A politician interviews every 8th grade student in the district to get the opinion of youth on a new policy.
b. A business directs users to leave anonymous reviews online.
c. A principal goes through the school directory and calls every 5th family to request opinions on a policy change.
d. A political commercial asks voters to call in with ideas for reform so that he can get a better understanding of what his constituents want.

16. What number should come next in the sequence: 3, 6, 8, 16, 18, 36, ...?

a. 38
b. 44
c. 57
d. 72

17. Which of these describes the graph of the equation $2x^2 - 3y^2 - 12x + 6y - 15 = 0$?

a. Circular
b. Elliptical
c. Parabolic
d. Hyperbolic

18. In a town of 6,089 people, about 80% of the population is over the age of 10. Of those, approximately 10% attend the local 4-year high school. If the number of students in each grade is about the same, how many 11th graders likely reside in the town?

a. Fewer than 100
b. Between 100 and 150
c. Between 150 and 200
d. More than 200

19. If $\cos\theta + 1 = 0$, which of the following is a possible value of θ?

a. -180°
b. -90°
c. 0°
d. 135°

20. A weight suspended on a spring is at its equilibrium point 6 inches above the top of a table. When the weight is pulled down 1.5 inches, it bounces above the equilibrium point and returns to the point from which it was released in 0.5 seconds. Which of these can be used to model the weight's height h above the table as a function of time t in seconds?

a. $h = -1.5\sin(2\pi t) + 6$
b. $h = -3\cos(\pi t) + 4.5$
c. $h = -1.5\cos(4\pi t) + 6$
d. $h = -3\cos(0.5\pi t) + 4.5$

21. A car is driving along the highway at a constant speed when it runs over a pebble, which becomes lodged in one of the tire's treads. If this graph represents the height h of the pebble above the road in inches (y-axis) as a function of time t in seconds (x-axis), which of these statements is true?

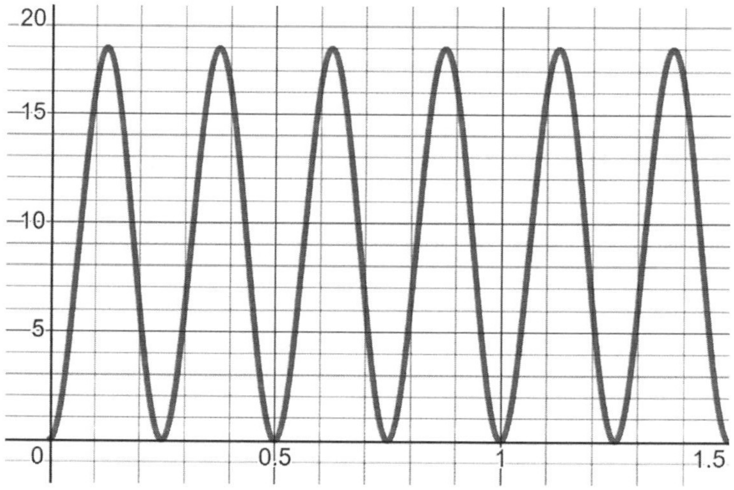

a. The outer radius of the tire is 9 inches, and the tire rotates 240 times per minute.
b. The outer radius of the tire is 18 inches, and the tire rotates 240 times per minute.
c. The outer radius of the tire is 9 inches, and the tire rotates 120 times per minute.
d. The outer radius of the tire is 18 inches, and the tire rotates 120 times per minute.

22. The graph of $f(x)$ is a parabola with a focus of $(a, 3)$ and a directrix of $y = -1$, and $g(x)$ represents a transformation of $f(x)$. If the vertex of the graph of $g(x)$ is $(a, 1)$, which of these is a possible equation for $g(x)$ for nonzero integers a and b?

a. $g(x) = f(x) + 3$
b. $g(x) = 2f(x)$
c. $g(x) = f(x + a)$
d. $g(x) = f(x - a) + 3$

23. Identify the cross-section polygon formed by a plane containing the given points on the cube.

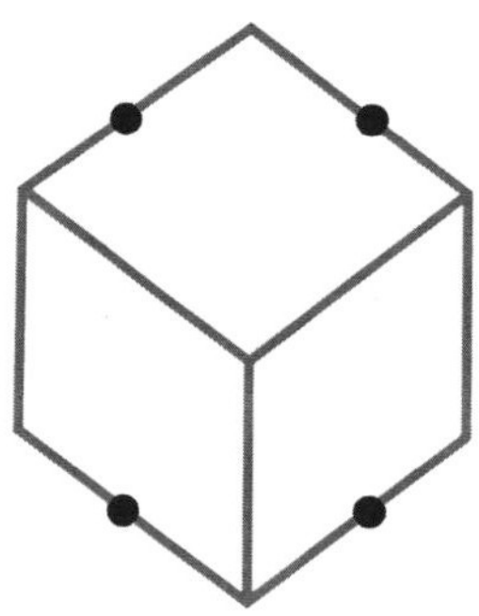

a. Rectangle
b. Trapezoid
c. Pentagon
d. Hexagon

24. If the diameter of Circle A is 12 cm and the radius of circle B is 15 cm, what is the ratio of the area of Circle A to the area of Circle B?

a. $\frac{4}{25}$
b. $\frac{16}{25}$
c. $\frac{2}{5}$
d. $\frac{4}{5}$

25. Natasha designs a square pyramidal tent for her children. Each of the sides of the square base measures x ft, and the tent's height is h feet. If Natasha were to increase by 1 ft the length of each side of the base, how much more interior space would the tent have?

a. $\frac{x^2h+2xh+h}{3}$ ft^3
b. $\frac{2xh+h}{3}$ ft^3
c. $\frac{x^2h+3}{3}$ ft^3
d. 1 ft^3

26. Which of the following piecewise functions can describe the graph below?

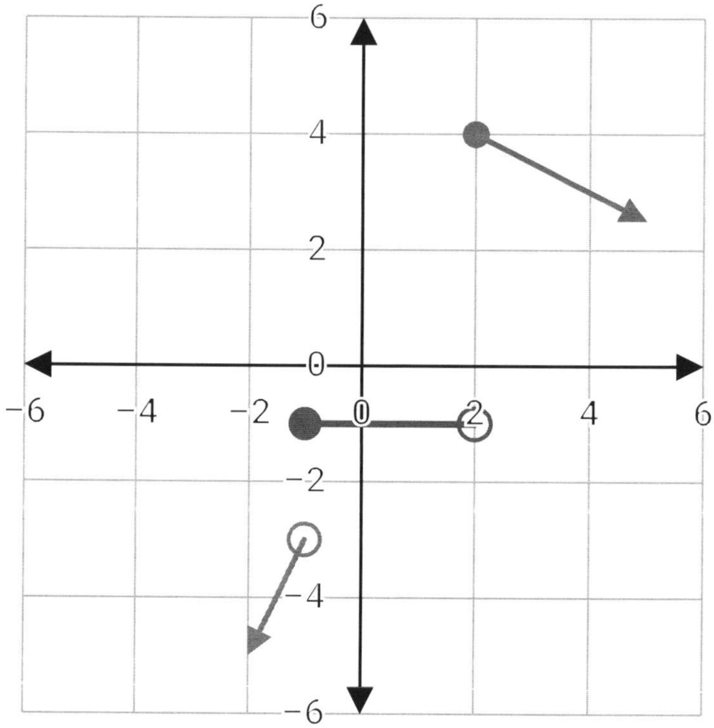

a. $f(x) = \begin{cases} 2x - 1 & x < -1 \\ -1 & -1 \leq x < 2 \\ -\frac{1}{2}x + 5 & x \geq 2 \end{cases}$

b. $f(x) = \begin{cases} 2x - 1 & x \leq -1 \\ [\![x]\!] & -1 \leq x \leq 2 \\ -x + 6 & x > 2 \end{cases}$

c. $f(x) = \begin{cases} 2x - 1 & x \leq -1 \\ -1 & -1 < x \leq 2 \\ -\frac{1}{2}x + 5 & x > 2 \end{cases}$

d. $f(x) = \begin{cases} x - 3 & x < -1 \\ -1 & -1 \leq x < 2 \\ -2x + 5 & x \geq 2 \end{cases}$

27. What is the exact value of tan $\left(-\frac{2\pi}{3}\right)$?

a. $-\sqrt{3}$
b. $\frac{\sqrt{3}}{3}$
c. 1
d. $\sqrt{3}$

28. Which of the following is a subset of the set of natural numbers?

a. Integers
b. Whole numbers
c. Prime numbers
d. Irrational numbers

29. What is the sum of the series $200 + 100 + 50 + 25 + \cdots$?

a. 375
b. 400
c. 600
d. The sum is infinite.

30. Two piano instructors compared notes on how long their students had been taking lessons. The charts below compare the two sets of data. Note: the instructors did not count the students who had been taking lessons for less than a year.

Which of the following is a true statement for these data?

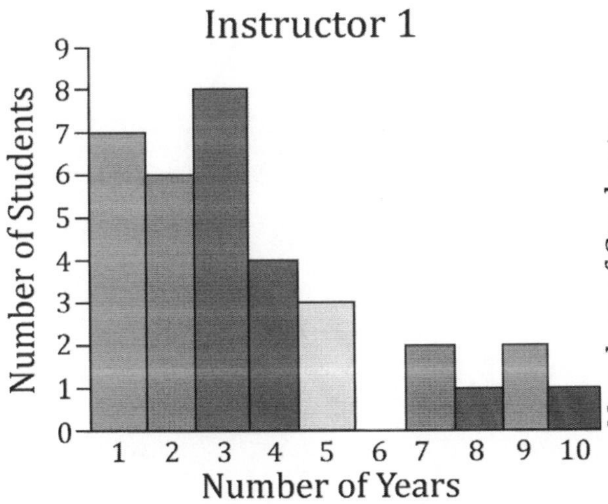

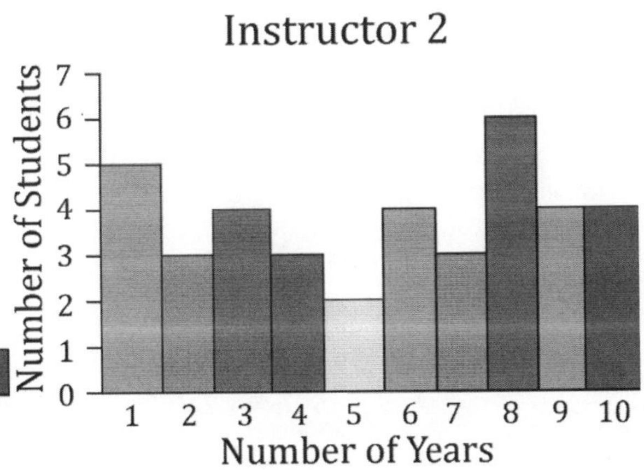

a. The median number of years a student has been taking lessons from Instructor 1 is five less than the median number for Instructor 2.
b. On average, students of Instructor 2 have been taking lessons for two years longer than students of Instructor 1 (round to the nearest whole number).
c. The mode number of years is higher for Instructor 1 than for Instructor 2.
d. The median number of years for Instructor 1 is greater than the mean.

31. Solve $x^4 + 225 = 34x^2$.

a. $x = \{3, 5\}$
b. $x = \{3i, 5i\}$
c. $x = \{-5, -3, 3, 5\}$
d. $x = \{-5i, -3i, 3i, 5i\}$

32. Which of the graphs shown represents $f(x) = 2|-x - 1| + 2$?

a.

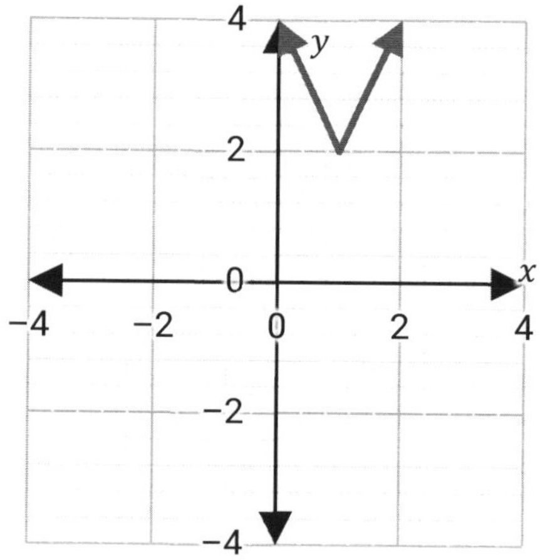

c.

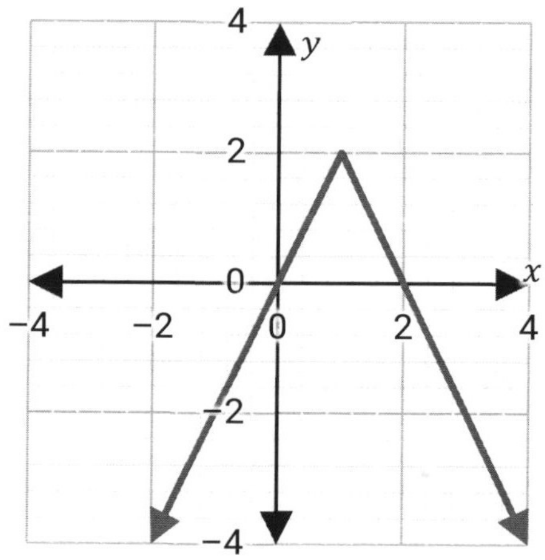

b.

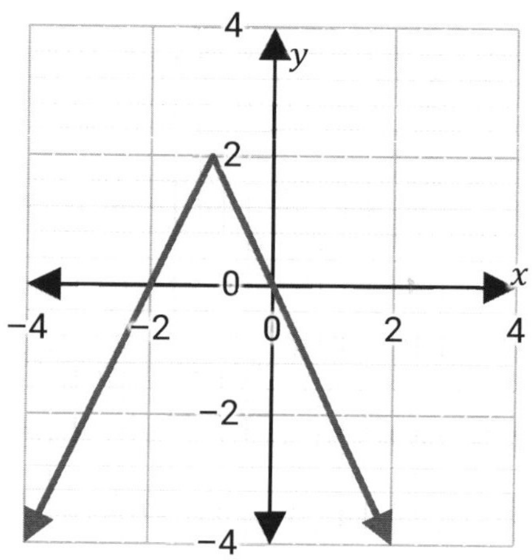

d.

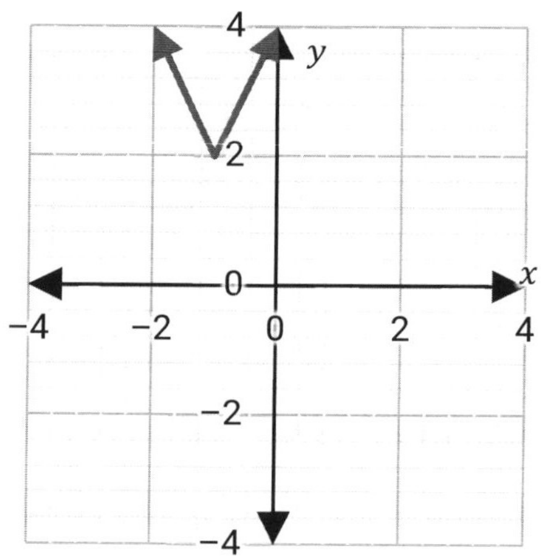

33. Which of these relationships represent y as a function of x?

a. $x = y^2$

c. $y = |x|$

b.

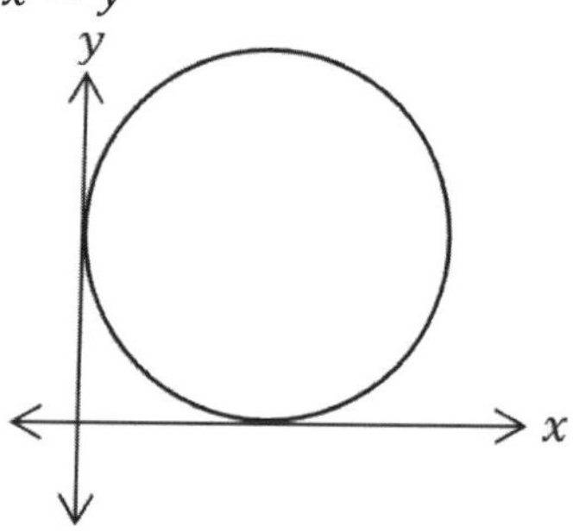

d.

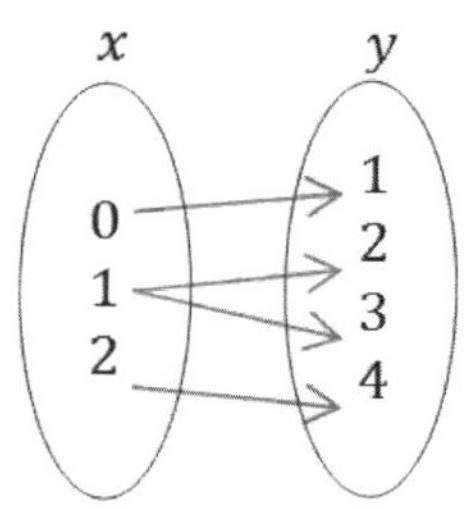

34. A triangle with vertices $A(-4,-3)$, $B(-2,0)$, and $C(-1,-1)$ is reflected across $y = x - 3$ to give $\Delta A'B'C'$, which is subsequently reflected across the y-axis to give $\Delta A''B''C''$. Which of these statements is true?

a. A translation of ΔABC three units up gives $\Delta A''B''C''$.
b. A reflection of ΔABC about the x-axis gives $\Delta A''B''C''$.
c. A 90° rotation of ΔABC about $(0,-3)$ gives $\Delta A''B''C''$.
d. A 270° rotation of ΔABC about $(0,-3)$ gives $\Delta A''B''C''$.

35. Starting at his house, Juan walks $(x - 10)$ meters west and x meters south to get to the park. On a neighborhood map that has a scale of 1 cm : 20 m, the straight-line distance between Juan's house and the park is 2.5 cm. How far did Juan walk to the park?

a. 30 m
b. 40 m
c. 50 m
d. 70 m

36. Two companies offer monthly cell phone plans, both of which include free text messaging. Company A charges a $25 monthly fee plus five cents per minute of phone conversation, while Company B charges a $50 monthly fee and offers unlimited calling. At what total duration of monthly calls do both companies charge the same amount?

a. 500 hours
b. 8 hours and 33 minutes
c. 8 hours and 20 minutes
d. 5 hours

37. A dress is marked down by 20% and placed on a clearance rack, under a sign reading "Take an extra 25% off already reduced merchandise." What fraction of the original price is the final sale price of the dress?

a. $\frac{2}{5}$
b. $\frac{9}{20}$
c. $\frac{3}{5}$
d. $\frac{11}{20}$

38. Oliver jogged to the park and then walked back home along the same route. It took him 30 minutes to jog to the park, and he walked home in an hour and a half, going 4 mph slower. What was Oliver's average speed on his round trip?

a. 3 mph
b. 3.5 mph
c. 4 mph
d. 4.5 mph

39. Which of these is the least biased sampling technique?

a. To assess his effectiveness in the classroom, a teacher distributes a teacher evaluation to all his students. Responses are anonymous and voluntary.
b. To determine the average intelligence quotient (IQ) of students in her school of 2,000 students, a principal uses a random number generator to select 300 students by student identification number and has them participate in a standardized IQ test.
c. To determine which video game is most popular among his fellow eleventh graders at school, a student surveys all the students in his English class.
d. Sixty percent of students at the school have a parent who is a member of the Parent-Teacher Association (PTA). To determine parent opinions regarding school improvement programs, the PTA requires submission of a survey response with membership dues.

40. Calculate: $\int 3x^2e^{x^3}\,dx$

a. $x^3e^{x^3} + C$
b. $e^{x^3} + C$
c. $x^3e^{\frac{x^4}{4}} + C$
d. $\ln x^3 + C$

41. Gene X has three possible alleles, or gene forms, called *a*, *b* and *c*. Each individual carries two copies of Gene X, one of which is inherited from his or her mother and the other of which is inherited from his or her father. If the two copies of Gene X are of the same form, the individual is homozygous for that allele; otherwise, the individual is heterozygous. The following table represents genetic data from 250 individuals selected at random from the population.

		Allele 2		
		a	*b*	*c*
Allele 1	*a*	5	8	24
	b	10	75	32
	c	18	52	26

Using experimental probability, predict the number of individuals in a population of 50,000 who will be heterozygous for the *b* allele.

a. 35,400
b. 20,400
c. 15,000
d. 3,600

42. Ava and Jack packed a picnic lunch and went for a hike. The graph below shows their distance from the start of the trail at times throughout the hike. If the x-axis represents the number of hours they spent and the y-axis represents their distance from the beginning of the trail in miles, which of the following statements is (are) true?

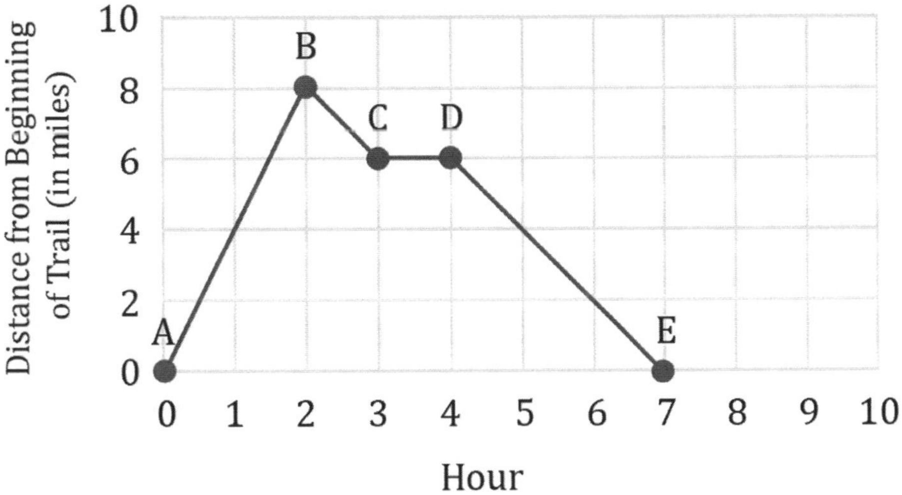

I. Their average speed was 4 mph.
II. Their speed from point B to point C was the same as from point D to E.
III. They walked a total distance of sixteen miles.

a. I only
b. II only
c. II and III
d. I, II, and III

43. The vertices of a polygon are $(0, 3)$, $(1, -1)$, $(3, 3)$, and $(4, -1)$. Which of the following describes the polygon most specifically?

a. Parallelogram
b. Rhombus
c. Rectangle
d. Square

44. If $3 \log_3 y + \log_3 3 = 4$, what is $\log_y 243$?

a. 3
b. 5
c. 6
d. 9

45. For ΔABC, what is the length of $\overline{AB}$?

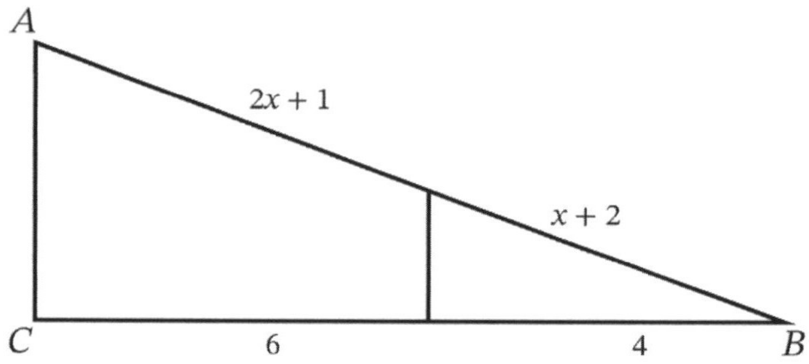

a. 4
b. 9
c. 12
d. 15

46. Which of these is a major contribution of the Arabic civilization to the historical development of mathematics?

a. The division of an hour into 60 minutes, and a minute into 60 seconds, and a circle into 360 degrees
b. The development of algebra as a discipline separate from geometry
c. The use of deductive reasoning in geometric proofs
d. The introduction of Boolean logic

47. Solve the system of equations: $\begin{cases} 3x + y = 1 \\ -4x + 3y = 29 \end{cases}$.

a. $(-2, 7)$
b. $(-1, 3)$
c. $\left(0, \frac{1}{2}\right)$
d. $\left(2, -\frac{5}{2}\right)$

48. Given the partial table of values for $f(x)$ and $g(x)$, find $f(g(3))$. Assume that $f(x)$ and $g(x)$ are the simplest polynomials that fit the data.

x	$f(x)$	$g(x)$
-2	-16	-11
-1	-2	-8
0	0	-5
1	2	-2
2	16	1

a. 169
b. 128
c. 72
d. 16

49. For which of these does a rotation of 120° about the center of the polygon map the polygon onto itself?

a. Square
b. Regular hexagon
c. Regular octagon
d. Regular decagon

50. Which of these statements is (are) true for the function $g(x)$?

$$g(x) = \begin{cases} x & x < 2 \\ -\frac{1}{2}x + 3 & x \geq 2 \end{cases}$$

I. $g(1) = 1$
II. The domain of $g(x)$ is all real numbers.
III. The range of $g(x)$ is $y \geq 2$.

a. II only
b. III only
c. I and II
d. I, II, and III

51. Solve $3x^3y^2 - 45x^2y = 15x^3y - 9x^2y^2$ for x and y.

a. $x = \{0, -3\}, y = \{0, 5\}$
b. $x = \{0\}, y = \{0\}$
c. $x = \{0, -3\}, y = \{0\}$
d. $x = \{0\}, y = \{0, 5\}$

52. Solve the system of equations.

$$\begin{cases} 2x - 4y + z = 10 \\ -3x + 2y - 4z = -7 \\ x + y - 3z = -1 \end{cases}$$

a. $(-1, -3, 0)$
b. $(-\frac{3}{4}, -\frac{21}{8}, -1)$
c. $(1, -2, 0)$
d. No solution

53. Given statements p and q, which of the following is the truth table for the statement:

$$q \leftrightarrow \neg(p \wedge q)$$

a.

p	q	$q \leftrightarrow \neg(p \wedge q)$
T	T	F
T	F	T
F	T	T
F	F	T

c.

p	q	$q \leftrightarrow \neg(p \wedge q)$
T	T	F
T	F	F
F	T	F
F	F	T

b.

p	q	$q \leftrightarrow \neg(p \wedge q)$
T	T	T
T	F	T
F	T	T
F	F	F

d.

p	q	$q \leftrightarrow \neg(p \wedge q)$
T	T	F
T	F	F
F	T	T
F	F	F

Refer to the following for questions 54–55:

The diagrams below show the number of people in a small town who participate in various types of volunteer work.

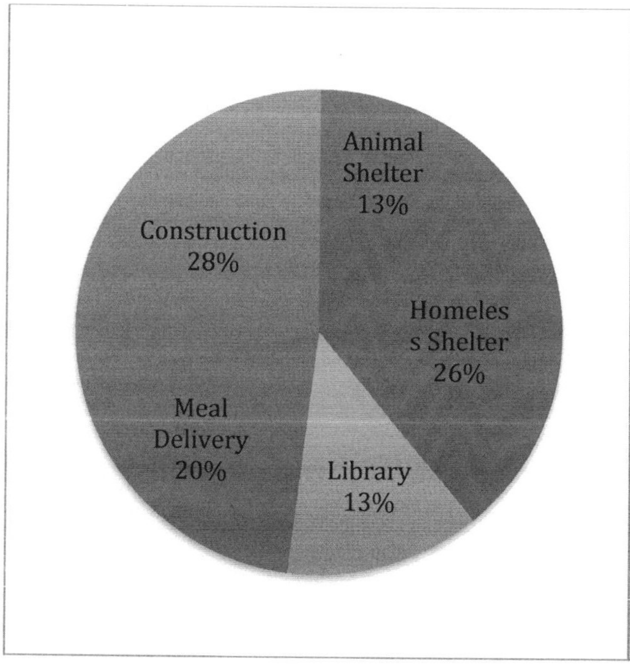

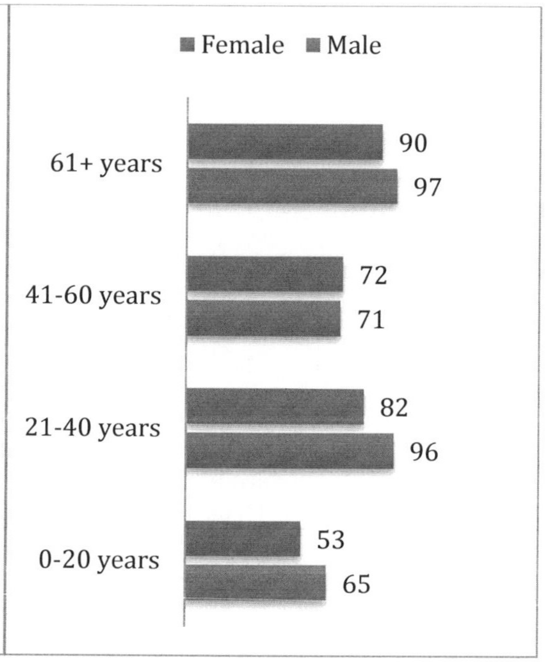

54. Which of these is the greatest quantity?

a. The average number of females per age bracket
b. The number of volunteers at the animal shelter
c. The difference in the number of male and female volunteers
d. The difference in the number of volunteers over age 60 and under age 21

55. A volunteer under age 21 is chosen at random for a scholarship. What is the approximate probability that the student is male?

a. 0.47
b. 0.51
c. 0.55
d. 0.58

56. Which of these is NOT a net of a rectangular prism?

a. 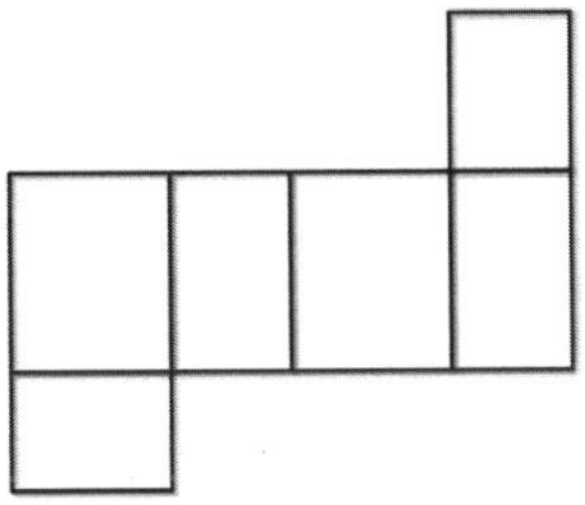

b. 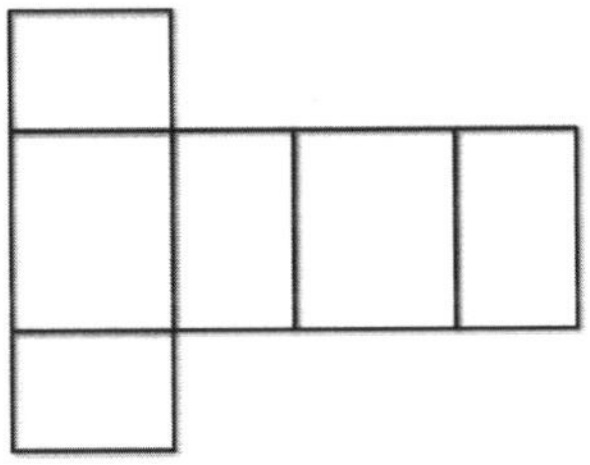

c. 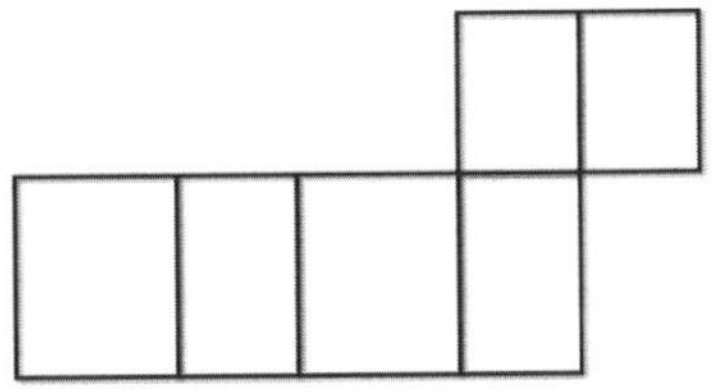

d. 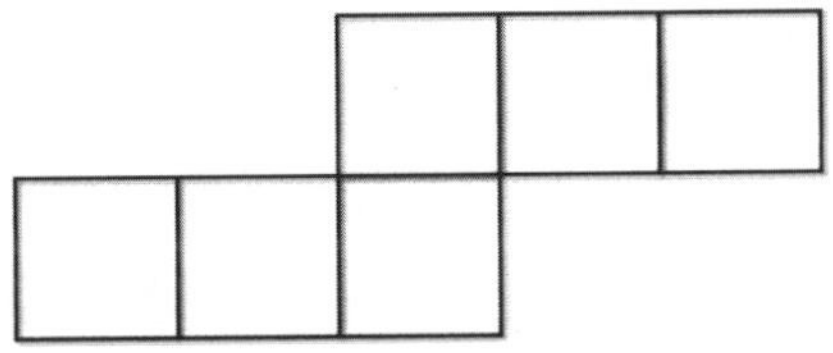

57. Which of these correctly defines the recursive sequence $a_1 = -1, a_{n+1} = a_n + 2$ explicitly?

a. $a_n = 2n - 3$
b. $a_n = -n + 2$
c. $a_n = n - 2$
d. $a_n = -2n + 3$

58. In how many distinguishable ways can a group of 7 be seated at a circular table?

a. 24
b. 120
c. 720
d. 5,040

59. If the square of three times the sum of a and six is fourteen more than a, which of these is a possible value of a?

a. $\sqrt{2}$
b. $\frac{3}{2}$
c. 1
d. -5

60. A colony of bacteria is grown in a lab. After 2 hours, the number of bacteria is determined to be 6×10^5. If the doubling time is 30 minutes, approximately how many bacteria should be counted after a total of 10 hours of growth from the start?

a. 2.6×10^8
b. 2.1×10^9
c. 3.9×10^{10}
d. 1.7×10^{11}

61. Bruce is attending a conference that is 827 km from his home. If he travels at a speed of 64 km/hour, approximately how long will it take him to reach his destination?

a. 5 hours
b. 9 hours
c. 13 hours
d. 17 hours

62. A target is made of concentric circles, as shown below. The width of each band is $2m$ and the center is a circle with radius of $2m$.

Which of the following gives the area of the two white rings as a function of m?

a. $A = 16\pi m^2$
b. $A = 24\pi m^2$
c. $A = 40\pi m^2$
d. $A = 64\pi m^2$

63. The high school honors program is offering three special electives: Biophysics, Intro to Law, and Latin. Seventeen students enrolled in Biophysics, twenty-two in Intro to Law, and nineteen in Latin. Two students are taking both Biophysics and Intro to Law, seven are taking both Intro to Law and Latin, and four are taking both Biophysics and Latin. One student enrolled in all three electives. How many students are taking special electives?

a. 46
b. 49
c. 55
d. 58

64. If a, b, and c are multiples of 6 and $3a^2 + 2b^3 = c$, of the following integers, which is the largest integer that must be factor of c?

a. 6
b. 36
c. 72
d. 108

65. A mountain climber climbs through rough terrain. She climbs 480 feet, 610 feet, 295 feet, and 303 feet over a period of 4 days. Estimate the distance she climbs over the four-day period to the nearest hundred feet.

a. 1,500 feet
b. 1,600 feet
c. 1,700 feet
d. 1,800 feet

66. Express the area of the given triangle as a function of x.

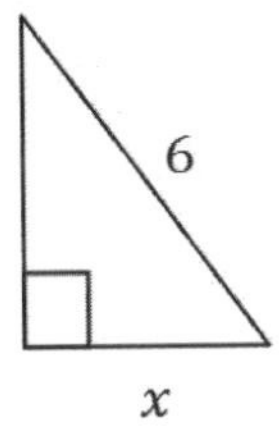

a. $A(x) = 3x$
b. $A(x) = \frac{x\sqrt{36-x^2}}{2}$
c. $A(x) = \frac{x^2}{2}$
d. $A(x) = 18 - \frac{x^2}{2}$

67. Simplify $\sqrt{\frac{-28x^6}{27y^5}}$.

a. $\frac{2x^3 i\sqrt{21y}}{9y^3}$
b. $\frac{2x^3 i\sqrt{21y}}{27y^4}$
c. $\frac{-2x^3\sqrt{21y}}{9y^3}$
d. $\frac{12x^3 yi\sqrt{7}}{27y^2}$

68. A rectangle has a length of 1299 cm and a width of 725 cm. Round each length to the nearest hundred centimeters and estimate the area of the rectangle.

a. 910,000 cm^2
b. 1,040,000 cm^2
c. 840,000 cm^2
d. 960,000 cm^2

69. Which of these is the equation of the function graphed below?

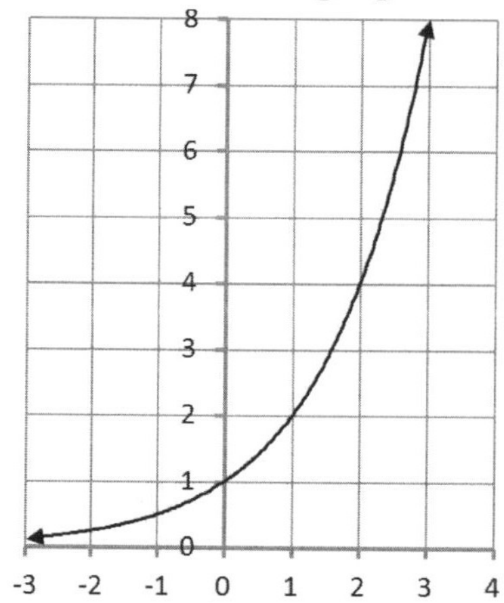

a. $f(x) = x^2$
b. $f(x) = \sqrt{x}$
c. $f(x) = 2^x$
d. $f(x) = \log_2 x$

70. A triangle has side lengths of 19.7 cm, 20.4 cm, and 10.2 cm. Round each length to the nearest ten centimeters and estimate the perimeter of the triangle.

a. 60 cm
b. 50 cm
c. 55 cm
d. 65 cm

71. If $f(x) = \tan(2x + 4)$, then $f^{-1}(x) =$

a. $\frac{1}{2}\tan^{-1}(x) - 2$
b. $\sec(2x + 4)$
c. $\tan^{-1}\left(\frac{1}{2}x - 2\right)$
d. $2\tan^{-1}(x) - 4$

72. A random sample of 250 students at a high school were asked these three questions:

Do you drink coffee?
Do you drink tea?
Do you drink hot chocolate?

The results of the survey are shown below. If these data are representative of the population of students at the school, which of these is most probable?

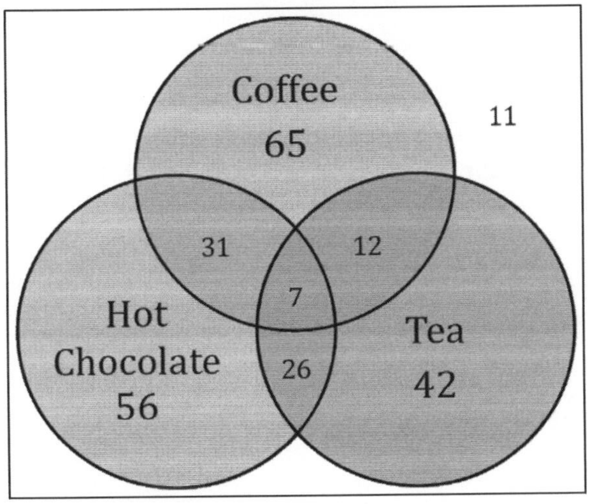

a. A student chosen at random drinks tea.
b. If a student chosen at random drinks hot chocolate, he also drinks at least one other beverage.
c. If a student chosen at random drinks coffee and hot chocolate, he also drinks tea.
d. A student chosen at random does not drink coffee, tea, or hot chocolate.

73. A farmer purchases 32 llamas to raise for their wool. The number of llamas on the farm each year is shown on the table below:

Years after purchase	0	1	2	3
Number of llamas	32	48	72	108

How many llamas should the farmer expect to have 4 years after the original purchase?

a. 144
b. 124
c. 132
d. 162

Refer to the following for question 74:

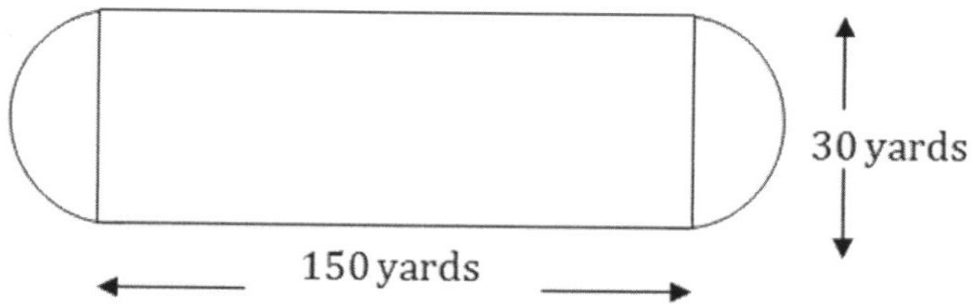

74. A company is building a track for a local high school. There are two straight sections and two semi-circular turns. Given the dimensions, which of the following most closely measures the perimeter of the entire track?

a. 180 yards
b. 300 yards
c. 360 yards
d. 395 yards

75. A cube inscribed in a sphere has a volume of 125 cubic units. What is the volume of the sphere in cubic units?

a. $25\pi\sqrt{3}$
b. $\frac{125\pi\sqrt{3}}{2}$
c. $\frac{375\pi\sqrt{3}}{8}$
d. $\frac{5\pi\sqrt{3}}{12}$

76. Marcus is putting chicken wire around his rectangular garden. He decides to add cantaloupes to his garden, so he needs to expand the size of the garden. He finds that by moving the boundary line back x feet on each of the four sides, he fences a rectangular space 34 yd^2 larger than the original plan and spends an extra \$36 on fencing, which costs \$1.50 per linear foot. How much does he spend?

a. \$145.50
b. \$171
c. \$223.50
d. \$352

77. On a floor plan drawn at a scale of 1: 150, the area of a rectangular room is 20 cm^2. What is the actual area of the room?

a. 4,500 cm^2
b. 45,000 cm^2
c. 45 m^2
d. 450 m^2

78. Which of the following expressions gives the area A of the triangle below in terms of x? Note: The figure is not drawn to scale.

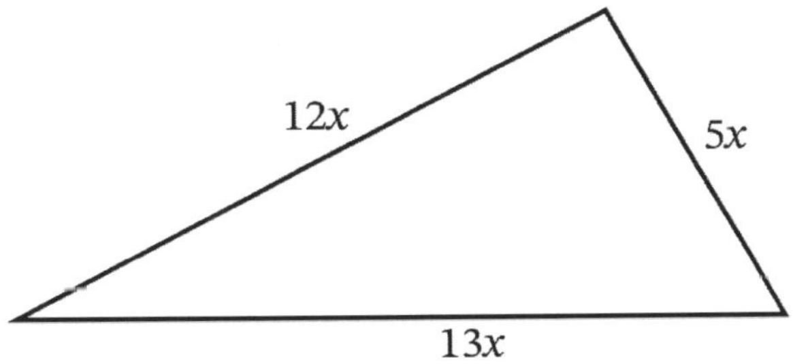

a. $30x^2$

b. $5\sqrt{3x^2 - 1}$

c. $\frac{x\sqrt{5x^2}}{12}$

d. $\frac{3x\sqrt{13x^2}}{25}$

79. If a, b, and c are even integers and $3a^2 + 9b^3 = c$, which of these is the largest number which must be factor of c?

a. 2

b. 3

c. 6

d. 12

Refer to the following for questions 80–81:

The box-and-whisker plot displays a district's standardized test scores by subject.

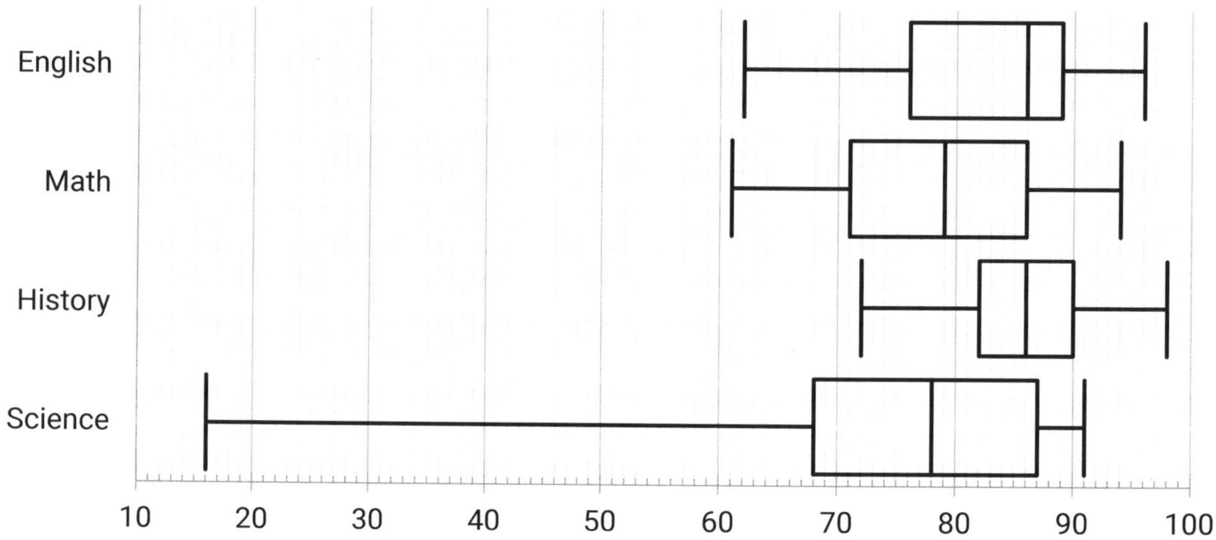

80. What is the probability that a student chosen at random from Math made above an 86 on this test?

a. 25%
b. 50%
c. 60%
d. 75%

81. Which of the following statements is NOT true of the data?

a. The median better reflects student performance in Science than the mean.
b. The mean test score for English and history is the same.
c. The median of the History scores is the same as the 3rd quartile score for Math.
d. The median test score is above the mean for English.

82. Simplify $(3 - 2i)^2 + (7 + 7i)$.

a. $\sqrt{119}$
b. $12 - 5i$
c. $12 + 5i$
d. 13

83. If $\sin\theta = \frac{\sqrt{2}}{2}$ when $\frac{\pi}{2} < \theta < \pi$, what is the value of θ?

a. $\frac{\pi}{4}$
b. $\frac{3\pi}{4}$
c. $\frac{2\pi}{3}$
d. $\frac{5\pi}{6}$

84. Which mathematician's name is used for the famous formula for solving right triangles $a^2+b^2 = c^2$?

a. Pythagoras
b. Euclid
c. Euler
d. Fermat

Refer to the following for question 85:

The box-and-whisker plot displays student test scores assessed throughout a semester to see if students were improving.

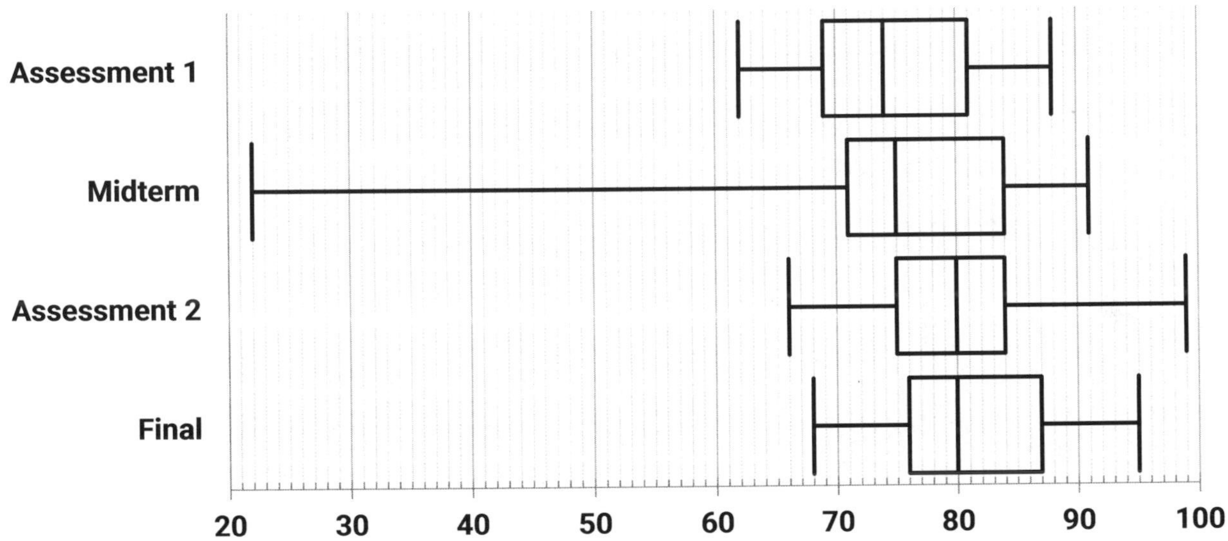

85. Which of the following statements is necessarily true of the data?

a. The mean better reflects student performance at the midterm than the median.
b. The mean test score for assessment 2 and the final is the same.
c. Assessment 1 had the highest median grade.
d. The median test score is below the mean for assessment 2.

86. Which of the following could be the graph of $y = -a(x+b)(x+c)^2$ if $a > 0$?

a.

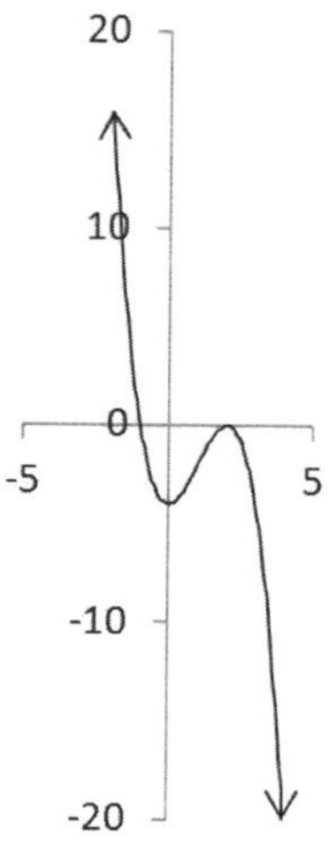

b.

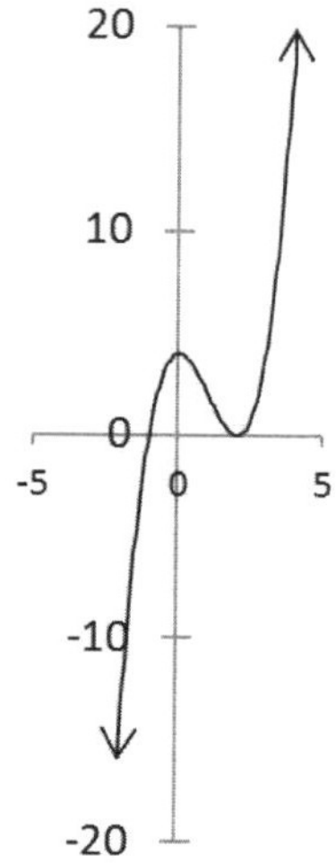

c.

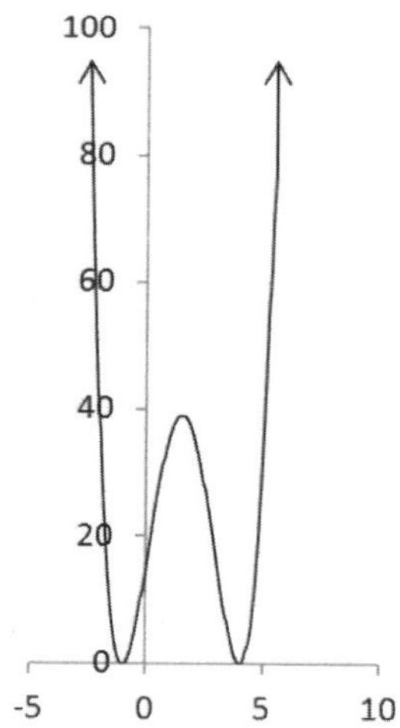

d.

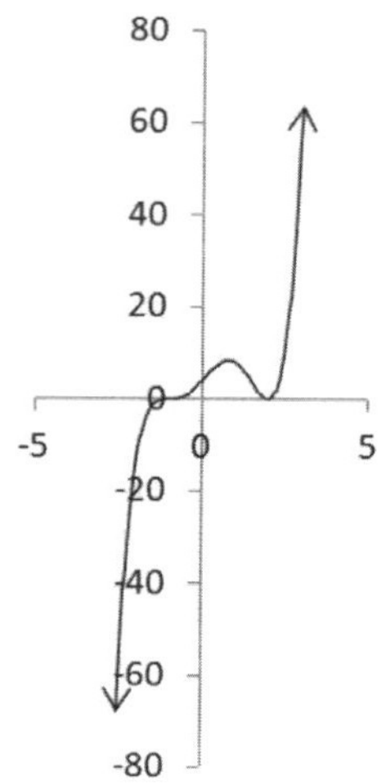

87. Solve the inequality: $|x+6| < 9$

a. $(-15, -3)$
b. $(-15, 3)$
c. $(3, -3)$
d. $(6, -9)$

88. In the figure below, $ABCD$ is a parallelogram. The angles are $m\angle A = (5x)°$ and $m\angle B = (2x-9)°$. Find $m\angle C$.

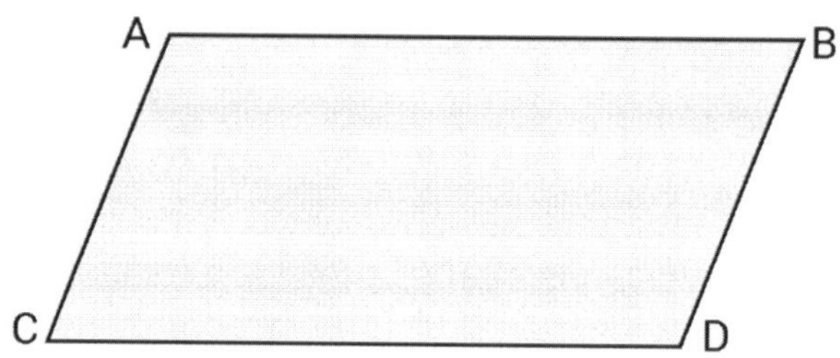

a. $m\angle C = 135°$
b. $m\angle C = 54°$
c. $m\angle C = 45°$
d. $m\angle C = 27°$

89. Which of these defines the recursive sequence $a_1 = -2$, $a_{n+1} = a_n + \frac{1}{2}$ explicitly?

a. $a_n = \frac{1}{2}n - 2$
b. $a_n = -2n + \frac{1}{2}$
c. $a_n = \frac{1}{2}n - \frac{5}{2}$
d. $a_n = -2n + \frac{5}{2}$

90. At today's visit to her doctor, Josephine was prescribed a liquid medication with instructions to take 25 cc's every four hours. She filled the prescription on her way to work, but when it came time to take the medicine, she realized that the pharmacist did not include a measuring cup. Josephine estimated that the plastic spoon in her desk drawer was about the same size as a teaspoon and decided to use it to measure the approximate dosage. She recalled that one cubic centimeter (cc) is equal to one milliliter (mL) but was not sure how many milliliters were in a teaspoon. So, she noted that a two-liter bottle of soda contains about the same amount as a half-gallon container of milk and applied her knowledge of the customary system of measurement to determine how many teaspoons of medicine to take. Which of these calculations might she have used to approximate her dosage?

a. $25 \times \frac{1}{1{,}000} \times \frac{2}{0.5} \times 16 \times 48$
b. $25 \times \frac{1}{100} \times \frac{0.5}{2} \times 16 \times 4 \times 12$
c. $\frac{1{,}000}{25} \times \frac{0.5}{2} \times 16 \times 4 \times 12$
d. $\frac{25}{1{,}000} \times \frac{1}{4} \times 16 \times 48$

91. Which of these does NOT simulate randomly selecting a student from a group of 8 students?

a. Creating an octagonal spinner, assigning each side to a different person, and spinning it
b. Assigning each student a unique coin flip value of HHH, HHT, HTH, THH, TTH, THT, HTT, or TTT and flipping a coin three times
c. Assigning each student a unique musical note A–G and blindly hitting a white key on a piano
d. Assigning each student a unique number 1-8 and randomly drawing from 8 numbered index cards

92. Given that x is a positive, even integer, y is a positive integer, and that the greatest common factor of x and y is greater than 1, which of the following are possibly true for Quantity A and Quantity B?

Quantity A	Quantity B
y	the least common multiple of x and y

I. Quantity A is greater
II. Quantity B is greater
III. The two quantities are the same

a. I
b. II
c. I and III
d. II and III

93. A high school club divides into 5 small groups for a service project. Each group has 4 girls and 4 boys. What is the total number of possible combinations in a single group?

a. 748,650
b. 1,225,000
c. 9,126,350
d. 23,474,025

94. Which of the following fractions is closest to $\frac{15,012}{19,938}$?

a. $\frac{1}{4}$
b. $\frac{3}{4}$
c. $\frac{4}{5}$
d. $\frac{5}{9}$

95. In ΔABC, if $\sin A = \cos 62°$, what is $\cos A$?

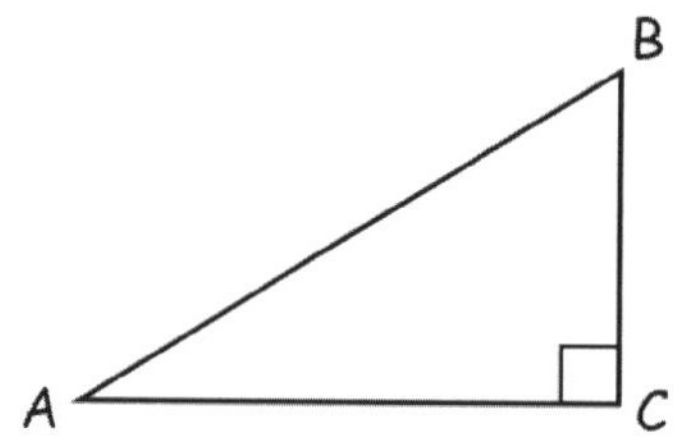

a. $\sin 28°$
b. $\sin 62°$
c. $\cos 62°$
d. $\sec 28°$

96. Attending a summer camp are 12 six-year-olds, 15 seven-year-olds, 14 eight-year-olds, 12 nine-year-olds, and 10 ten-year-olds. If a camper is randomly selected to participate in a special event, what is the probability that he or she is at least eight years old?

a. $\frac{2}{9}$
b. $\frac{22}{63}$
c. $\frac{4}{7}$
d. $\frac{3}{7}$

97. The intelligence quotients (IQs) of a randomly selected group of 300 people are normally distributed with a mean IQ of 100 and a standard deviation of 15. In a normal distribution, approximately 68% of values are within one standard deviation of the mean. About how many individuals from the selected group have IQs of at least 85?

a. 96
b. 200
c. 216
d. 252

98. Simplify: $\frac{(x^2y)(2xy^{-2})^3}{16x^5y^2} + \frac{3}{xy}$.

a. $\frac{3x+24y^6}{8xy^7}$
b. $\frac{x+6y^6}{2xy^7}$
c. $\frac{x+24y^5}{8xy^6}$
d. $\frac{x+6y^5}{2xy^6}$

99. If the midpoint of a line segment graphed on the xy-coordinate plane is $(1, -4)$ and the slope of the line segment is 3, which of these is a possible endpoint of the line segment?

a. $(-3, -16)$
b. $(2, -7)$
c. $(-1, 4)$
d. $(5, 9)$

100. Solve $\frac{x-2}{x-1} = \frac{x-1}{x+1} + \frac{2}{x-1}$.

a. $x = 2$
b. $x = -5$
c. $x = 1$
d. No solution

Answer Key and Explanations for Test #1

1. C: Aaron ran four miles from home and then back again, so he ran a total of eight miles. Therefore, statement III is false. Statements I and II, however, are both true. Since Aaron ran eight miles in eighty minutes, he ran an average of 1 mile every 10 minutes, or 6 miles every 60 minutes, which is 6 mph. He ran two miles from point (A) to (B) in 20 minutes, which is a rate of 1 mile per 10 minutes, and four miles from (D) to (E) in 40 minutes, which is also a rate of 1 mile per 10 minutes, so his running speed between both sets of points was the same.

2. D: Percent error $= \frac{|\text{actual value} - \text{measured value}|}{\text{actual value}} \times 100\%$, and the average percent error is the sum of the percent errors for each trial divided by the number of trials.

	Percent Error Trial 1	Percent Error Trial 2	Percent Error Trial 3	Percent Error Trial 4	Average Percent Error
Scale 1	1.4%	1.32%	1.36%	1.4%	1.37%
Scale 2	0.2%	0.28%	0.08%	0.12%	0.17%

The percent error for Scale 2 is less than the percent error for Scale 1, so it is more accurate. The more precise scale is Scale 1 because its range of values, 24.65 g − 24.67 g = 0.02 g, is smaller than Scale 2's range of values, 24.95 g − 25.07 g = 0.12 g.

3. E: First, we must determine the total amount of money Krystal spent. To do so, we must add the cost of the sunglasses, $19.99, and the scarf, $27.50. To add decimals, we stack the numbers so that the decimal points are directly on top of one another. Then, we add using the traditional algorithm, bringing the decimal point straight down into our sum. This gives us a total cost of $47.49. To determine Krystal's change, we must subtract our total, $47.49, from $50.00. Again, we must be sure to stack our decimal points directly on top of one another. Then we subtract as normal, bringing our decimal point straight down into our answer. We need to be careful that we borrow when necessary. The difference of $50.00 and $47.49 is $2.51. Krystal will receive change in the amount of $2.51.

4. C: In the box-and-whisker plot in choice A, the lowest value is 3, which is much too low, so choice A is not representative of the data from the stem and leaf plot.

To draw a pie chart, find the percentage of data contained in each of the ranges shown. There are 5 out of 20 numbers between 10 and 19, inclusive, so the percentage shown in the pie chart for that range of data is $\frac{5}{20} \times 100\% = 25\%$; there are 3 values between 20 and 29, inclusive, so the percentage of data for that sector is $\frac{3}{20} \times 100\% = 15\%$. Since the pie chart shows 30% for the 20–29 range, choice B is not representative of the data.

To draw a cumulative frequency histogram, find the cumulative frequency of the data.

Range	Frequency	Cumulative Frequency
10–19	5	5
20–29	3	8
30–39	6	14
40–49	6	20

The histogram shows the correct cumulative frequencies.

The data points in the line graph in choice D do not correspond to the data points given for the question.

5. B: If the three triangles are congruent and isosceles, the two base angles in each triangle are congruent. The interior angles of a triangle add to 180°. Therefore, $0.5x + 12 + 0.5x + 12 + x = 180$. Solve for x.

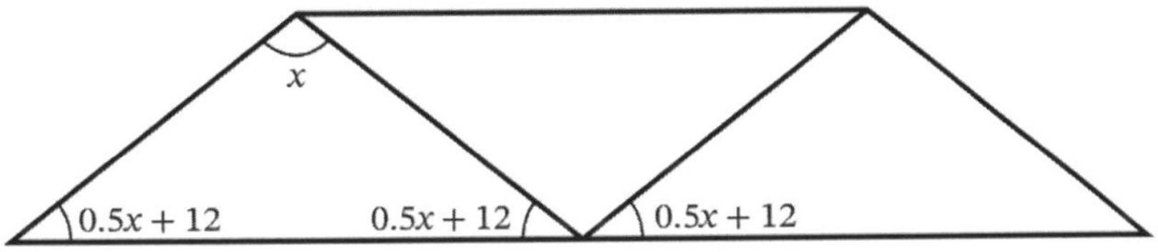

$$\begin{aligned} 0.5x + 12 + 0.5x + 12 + x &= 180 \\ 2x + 24 &= 180 \\ 2x &= 156 \\ x &= 78 \end{aligned}$$

Therefore, the value of x is 78.

6. C: The problem does not give any information about the size of the table or the spacing between any of the chairs. Nevertheless, creating a simple illustration that shows the order of the chairs will help when approaching this problem. The line below shows the row of chairs and possible positions based on the parameters.

Statements I and III seem to be true from the drawing, but since we are not given any information about the spacing between chairs, we cannot say definitively that H and L are farther apart than I and M, or that M and K are closer together than H and L. If the statement would have talked about the number of chairs between rather than distance, the statements would have also been true. However, we do know that chair I is between chairs J and L, so the only statement that is necessarily true is statement II.

7. D: Set the given expression equal to y, then solve for y. When $y = \frac{1}{\sqrt{x}}$, $x = \frac{1}{y^2}$ or y^{-2}. Similarly, when $y = \cos x$, $x = \cos^{-1} y$. On the other hand, when $y = 2x$, $x = \frac{y}{2}$; when $y = e^x$, $x = \ln y$ for $y > 0$; and when $y = \frac{1}{x^2}$, $x = \pm\sqrt{\frac{1}{y}}$.

8. B: This problem can be solved using proportions. Determine the number of feet between the two points by setting up the following proportion.

$$\frac{1 \text{ in}}{10 \text{ ft}} = \frac{24 \text{ in}}{x \text{ ft}}$$

Cross multiply to solve for x.

$$1 \times x = 24 \times 10$$
$$x = 240$$

Therefore, the two points are 240 feet apart. From here, convert 240 feet to a distance in yards. To do so, multiply by the conversion factor $\frac{1 \text{ yd}}{3 \text{ ft}}$.

$$240 \text{ ft} \times \frac{1 \text{ yd}}{3 \text{ ft}} = 80 \text{ yd}$$

The two points are 80 yards apart.

9. B: We can sketch a quick diagram of the password to be filled in:

$$\_\ \_\ \_\ \_\ \_\ \_$$

The first two characters are unique letters, so they do not repeat. Thus, there are 26 options for the first slot and 25 for the second.

$$26\ \ 25\ \ \_\ \_\ \_\ \_$$

For the digits, we start with the final one, because it has the most restrictions, and then fill in the remaining three slots. There are five odd numbers, so we place a 5 in the final blank. That leaves nine unique numbers for the next slot, eight for the one after that, and seven for the final slot:

$$26\ \ 25\ \ 9\ \ 8\ \ 7\ \ 5$$

Finally, we multiply the six numbers together to find the number of possible passwords:

$$26 \times 25 \times 9 \times 8 \times 7 \times 5 = 1{,}638{,}000$$

10. C: First, multiply the numerator and denominator by the denominator's conjugate, $3 - 2i$. Then, simplify the result and write the answer in the form $a + bi$.

$$\begin{aligned} \frac{2-5i}{3+2i} \times \frac{3-2i}{3-2i} &= \frac{6-4i-15i+10i^2}{9-4i^2} \\ &= \frac{6-19i-10}{9+4} \\ &= \frac{-4-19i}{13} \\ &= -\frac{4}{13} - \frac{19}{13}i \end{aligned}$$

11. D: First, state the exclusions of the domain.

$$x^3 - 7x + 6 \neq 0$$
$$(x+3)(x-1)(x-2) \neq 0$$
$$x+3 \neq 0 \quad x-1 \neq 0 \quad x-2 \neq 0$$
$$x \neq -3 \quad x \neq 1 \quad x \neq 2$$

To determine whether there are asymptotes or holes at these values of x, simplify the expression:

$$\frac{x^2 - x - 2}{x^3 - 7x + 6} = \frac{(x-2)(x+1)}{(x+3)(x-1)(x-2)} = \frac{x+1}{(x+3)(x-1)}$$

There are asymptotes at $x = 1$ and at $x = -3$ and a hole at $x = 2$. Statement I is false.

To find the x-intercept of $f(x)$, solve $f(x) = 0$. $f(x) = 0$ when the numerator is equal to zero. The numerator equals zero when $x = 2$ and $x = -1$; however, 2 is excluded from the domain of $f(x)$, so the x-intercept is -1. This is enough to say statement II is false. To find the y-intercept of $f(x)$, find $f(0)$.

$$f(0) = \frac{0^2 - 0 - 2}{0^3 - 7(0) + 6} = \frac{-2}{6} = -\frac{1}{3}$$

The y-intercept is $-\frac{1}{3}$, but the x-intercept is not $-\frac{1}{3}$. Statement II is false.

12. A: Setting the cost of shipping equal to the amount received gives us the equation $3{,}000 + 100x = 400x$. Subtract $100x$ from both sides to get $3{,}000 = 300x$, then divide both sides by 300 to see that $x = 10$. Therefore, the least number of computers that must be shipped and sold is 10.

13. C: Since each coin toss is an independent event, the probability of the compound event of flipping the coin three times is equal to the product of the probabilities of the individual events. For example, $P(HHH) = P(H) \times P(H) \times P(H)$, $P(HHT) = P(H) \times P(H) \times P(T)$, etc. When a coin is flipped three times, all of the possible outcomes are HHH, HHT, HTH, HTT, THH, THT, TTH, and TTT. Using the data from the all heads and all tails results, calculate an experimental probability $P(H)$:

$$\begin{aligned} P(\text{three heads}) &= P(HHH) \\ &= P(H) \times P(H) \times P(H) \\ &= [P(H)]^3 \\ [P(H)]^3 &= \frac{30}{100} \\ [P(H)] &= \sqrt[3]{0.3} \approx 0.67 \end{aligned}$$

$$\begin{aligned} P(\text{no heads}) &= P(TTT) \\ &= P(T) \times P(T) \times P(T) \\ &= [P(T)]^3 \\ [P(T)]^3 &= \frac{4}{100} \\ [P(T)] &= \sqrt[3]{0.04} \approx 0.34 \\ P(H) &= 1 - P(T) \approx 0.66 \end{aligned}$$

Notice that these calculated values of $P(H)$ are approximately the same. Since 100 is a fairly large sample size for this kind of experiment, the approximation for $P(H)$ ought to be consistent for the compiled data set. Rather than calculating $P(H)$ using the data for one head and two heads, use the average calculated probability to confirm that the number of expected outcomes of one head and two head matches the number of actual outcomes.

$$P(\text{one head}) = P(HTT) + P(THT) + P(TTH) = 3 \times P(H) \times P(T) \times P(T) = 3 \times P(H) \times [P(T)]^2$$

$$P(\text{two heads}) = P(HHT) + P(HTH) + P(THH) = 3 \times P(H) \times P(H) \times P(T) = 3 \times [P(H)]^2 \times P(T)$$

The number of expected outcomes of getting one head in three coin flips out of 100 trials $100\{3(0.665)[(1-0.665)^2]\} \approx 22$, and the expected outcome getting of two heads in three coin flips out of 100 trials three flips is $100\{3(0.665)^2(1-0.665)\} \approx 44$. Since 22 and 44 are, in fact, the data obtained, 0.665 is indeed a good approximation for $P(H)$ when the coin used in this experiment is tossed.

14. D: A fair coin has a symmetrical binomial distribution which peaks in its center. Since choice C shows a skewed distribution for the fair coin, it cannot be the correct answer. From the frequency histogram given for the misshapen coin, it is evident that the misshapen coin is more likely to land on heads. Therefore, it is more likely that 10 coin flips would result in fewer tails than 10 coin flips of a fair coin; consequently, the probability distribution for the misshapen coin would be higher than the fair coin's distribution toward the smaller number of tails. Choice A shows a probability distribution which peaks at a value of 5 and which is symmetrical with respect to the peak, which verifies that it cannot be correct. Furthermore, in choice A, the sum of the probabilities shown for each number of tails for the misshapen coin is not equal to 1. The distribution for the misshapen coin in choice B is skewed in the wrong direction, favoring tails instead of heads, and must therefore also be incorrect. Choice D shows the correct binomial distribution for the fair coin and the appropriate shift for the misshapen coin.

15. C: Choice A represents convenience sampling since it is limited to one age. The pool of 8th grade students may not represent the opinions of all youth in the district. Choice B is biased because participants are self-selected rather than randomly selected. It may be that customers who have a strong opinion are more likely to respond than those who are more neutral, and this would give a skewed perspective of opinions. In choice C, families are randomly selected, so the sampling technique is not biased. Choice D, like choice B, is biased because participants are self-selected rather than randomly selected.

16. A: In this sequence, each number is either double the preceding number or 2 more than the preceding number, and these procedures alternate. Since $36 = 2 \times 18$, the next element of the sequence will be determined by adding 2. Since $36 + 2 = 38$, the next number in the sequence is 38.

17. D: One way to determine whether the equation represents an ellipse, a circle, a parabola, or a hyperbola is to find the discriminant $b^2 - 4ac$ of the general equation form of a conic section, $ax^2 + bxy + cy^2 + dx + ey + f = 0$, where a, b, c, d, e, and f are constants. Given that the conic section is non-degenerate, if the discriminant is positive, then the equation is a hyperbola; if the discriminant is negative, then the equation is a circle (when $a = c$ and $b = 0$) or an ellipse; and if the discriminant is zero, then the equation is a parabola. For $2x^2 - 3y^2 - 12x + 6y - 15 = 0$, $a = 2, b = 0, c = -3, d = -12, e = 6$, and $f = -15$. The discriminant $b^2 - 4ac$ is equal to $0^2 - 4(2)(-3) = 24$. Since the discriminant is positive, the graph is hyperbolic.

18. B: The population is approximately 6,000, so 80% of the population consists of about 4,800 individuals over age 10. Ten percent of 4,800 is 480, the approximate number of students in the local high school. Since there are four grades, there are about 120 students in each grade. So, the number of 11th graders is likely between 100 and 150.

19. A: If $\cos\theta + 1 = 0$, then $\cos\theta = -1$. This has only one solution in the interval $0° \leq \theta < 360°$, namely $\theta = 180°$. This is not one of the answer choices; however, the cosine function has a period of 360°, which means that adding or subtracting any multiple of 360° to the argument does not change the result. Since $180° - 360° = -180°$, $\cos(-180°) = \cos(180°) = -1$, so -180° is also a solution to the equation.

20. C: The movement of the weight can be described by graphing height h in inches as a function of time t in seconds. Notice that the height is 4.5 in above the table at time 0 since the weight was pulled down 1.5 inches from its starting position 6 inches above the table. The spring fluctuates 1.5 inches above and below its equilibrium point, so its maximum height is 7.5 inches above the table. The graph represents a cosine curve that has been inverted, stretched vertically by a factor of 1.5, and shifted up 6 units; also, the graph has been compressed horizontally, with a period of 0.5 rather than 2π. So, the height of the weight on the spring as a function of time is $h = -1.5\cos(4\pi t) + 6$.

21. A: Since the graph shows a maximum height of 18 inches above the ground, and since the maximum distance from the road the pebble reaches occurs when it is at the top of the tire, the diameter of the tire is 18 inches. Therefore, its radius is 9 inches. From the graph, it can be observed that the tire makes 6 rotations in 1.5 seconds. Thus, the tire rotates 4 times in 1 second, or $4 \times 60 = 240$ times per minute.

22. B: The graph of $f(x)$ is a parabola with a focus of $(a, 3)$ and a directrix of $y = -1$. The axis of symmetry of a parabola passes through the focus and vertex and is perpendicular to the directrix. Since the directrix is a horizontal line, the axis of symmetry is $x = a$; therefore, the x-coordinate of the parabola's vertex must be a. The distance between a point on the parabola and the directrix is equal to the distance between that point and the focus, so the y-coordinate of the vertex must be $y = \frac{-1+3}{2} = 1$. So, the vertex of the parabola given by $f(x)$ is $(a, 1)$.

If $g(x)$ were a translation of $f(x)$, as is the case for choices B, C, and D, the vertices of $f(x)$ and $g(x)$ would differ. Since the vertex of the graph of $g(x)$ is $(a, 1)$, none of those choices represent the correct response. However, if $g(x) = 2f(x)$, the vertices of the graphs of both functions would be the same; therefore, this represents a possible relation between the two functions.

23. D: The cross-section is a hexagon.

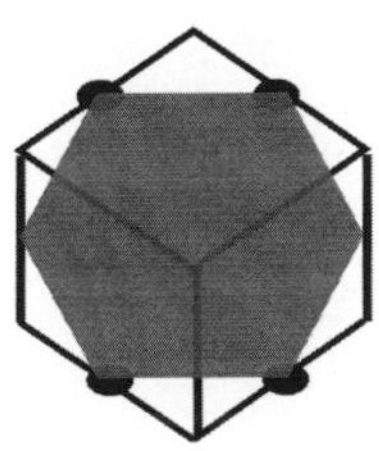

24. A: The area of each circle can be found by the formula $A = \pi r^2$. The radius of Circle A is half the diameter, or 6 cm, so the area of Circle A is $\pi(6)^2 = 36\pi$. The radius of Circle B is 15 cm, so the area of Circle B is $\pi(15)^2 = 225\pi$. The ratio of Circle A to Circle B is $\frac{36\pi}{225\pi} = \frac{36}{225} = \frac{4}{25}$. Answer B is the ratio of the areas of the two circles if both given measurements are treated as the diameter or as the radius, rather than one of each. Answer C is the ratio of the circumferences of the two circles.

Answer D is the ratio of the circumferences of the two circles if both given measurements are treated as the diameter or as the radius, rather than one of each.

25. B: The volume of Natasha's tent can be found by using the volume formula for a square pyramid, $V = \frac{1}{3}Bh = \frac{1}{3}s^2h$, where B is the area of the base, s is the side length of the square base, and h is the height of the pyramid. Therefore, the volume of her tent is $\frac{x^2h}{3}$. If she were to increase the length of each side of the square base by 1 ft, the tent's volume would be $\frac{(x+1)^2h}{3} = \frac{(x^2+2x+1)(h)}{3} = \frac{x^2h+2xh+h}{3} = \frac{x^2h}{3} + \frac{2xh+h}{3}$. Notice this is the volume of Natasha's tent, $\frac{x^2h}{3}$, increased by $\frac{2xh+h}{3}$.

26. A: In the range $(-\infty,-1)$, the graph represented is $y = 2x - 1$. In the range $[-1,2)$, the graph is $y = -1$. In the range $[2,\infty)$, the graph is $y = -\frac{1}{2}x + 5$.

27. D: The angle $-\frac{2\pi}{3}$ is equivalent to $2\pi - \frac{2\pi}{3} = \frac{4\pi}{3}$.

$$\tan\left(-\frac{2\pi}{3}\right) = \tan\left(\frac{4\pi}{3}\right) = \frac{\sin\left(\frac{4\pi}{3}\right)}{\cos\left(\frac{4\pi}{3}\right)}$$

From the unit circle, the values of $\sin\left(\frac{4\pi}{3}\right)$ and $\cos\left(\frac{4\pi}{3}\right)$ are $-\frac{\sqrt{3}}{2}$ and $-\frac{1}{2}$, respectively. Substitute these values into the equation from above.

$$\tan\left(-\frac{2\pi}{3}\right) = \frac{-\frac{\sqrt{3}}{2}}{-\frac{1}{2}} = -\frac{\sqrt{3}}{2} \times -\frac{2}{1} = \sqrt{3}$$

Therefore, the value of $\tan\left(-\frac{2\pi}{3}\right)$ is $\sqrt{3}$.

28. C: The set of prime numbers is a subset of the set of natural numbers, but the set of natural numbers is a subset of both the set of integers and the set of whole numbers.

29. B: The series is an infinite geometric series, the sum of which can be found by using the formula $\sum_{n=0}^{\infty} ar^n = \frac{a}{1-r}$, $|r| < 1$ where a is the first term in the series and r is the ratio between successive terms. In the series $200 + 100 + 50 + 25 + \cdots$, $a = 200$ and $r = \frac{1}{2}$. So, the sum of the series is:

$$\frac{200}{1-\frac{1}{2}} = \frac{200}{\frac{1}{2}} = 400$$

30. B: Instructor 1 has 34 students, so the median number of years is the average of the 17th and 18th student. These students have both been taking lessons for 3 years, so the median is 3. Instructor 2 has 38 students, so the median number of years is the average of the 19th and 20th student. These students have both been taking lessons for 6 years, so the median is 6. Since $6 - 3 = 3$, the median number of years a student has been taking lessons from Instructor 1 is three less than the median number for Instructor 2.

To find the mean, find the sum of the number of years and divide by the number of students. If the frequency of students who have been taking lessons for one year is 7, the number 1 is added seven times (1×7), if frequency for two years is 6, the number 2 is added six times (2×6), and so on. Divide the sum of these products by the number of students to find the mean. For Instructor 1, the mean is 3.65 years, which rounds up to 4 years. For Instructor 2, the mean is 5.63, which rounds up to 6 years. So, the students of Instructor 2 have been taking lessons for two years longer than the students of Instructor 1, on average.

The mode is the number of years for which the frequency is the highest. For Instructor 1, the mode is 3 years, and for Instructor 2, the mode is 8 years.

As seen above, the median for Instructor 1 is 3 and the mean is 3.65, so the median is less than the mean.

31. C: One way to solve the equation is to write $x^4 + 225 = 34x^2$ in the following form.

$$x^4 - 34x^2 + 225 = 0$$

This trinomial can be factored as $(x^2 - 9)(x^2 - 25) = 0$. In each set of parentheses is a difference of squares, which can be factored further: $(x + 3)(x - 3)(x + 5)(x - 5) = 0$. Use the zero-product property to find the solutions to the equation.

$x + 3 = 0$	$x - 3 = 0$	$x + 5 = 0$	$x - 5 = 0$
$x = -3$	$x = 3$	$x = -5$	$x = 5$

Therefore, the solution to the equation is $x = \{-5, -3, 3, 5\}$.

32. D: One way to determine which is the graph of $f(x) = 2|-x - 1| + 2$ is to find $f(x)$ for a few values of x. For example, $f(0) = 2|0 - 1| + 2 = 4$. Graphs A and D pass through (0,4), but graphs B and C do not. $f(-1) = 2|1 - 1| + 2 = 2$. Graphs B and D pass through $(-1,2)$, but graphs A and C do not. Graph D is the correct graph.

33. C: Choice C is the equation for an absolute value function. A function is a relationship in which for every element of the domain (x), there is exactly one element of the range (y). Graphically, a relationship between x and y can be identified as a function if the graph passes the vertical line test. The absolute value function passes this test.

The first relation is a parabola on its side, which fails the vertical line test for functions. A circle (choice B) also fails the vertical line test and is therefore not a function. The relation in choice D pairs two elements of the range with one of the elements of the domain, so it is also not a function.

34. C: When a figure is reflected twice over non-parallel lines, the resulting transformation is a rotation about the point of intersection of the two lines of reflection. The two lines of reflection $y = x - 3$ and $x = 0$ intersect at $(0, -3)$. So, $\Delta A''B''C''$ represents a rotation of ΔABC about the point $(0, -3)$. The angle of rotation is equal to twice the angle between the two lines of reflection when measured in a counterclockwise direction from the first to the second line of reflection. Since the angle between the lines or reflection measures 45°, the angle of rotation equivalent to the composition of the two reflections measures 90°.

35. D: If the distance is 2.5 cm on the map, then the actual distance is 2.5 cm $\times \frac{20\text{ m}}{1\text{ cm}} = 50$ m. To find x, use the Pythagorean theorem, then solve the resulting quadratic equation.

$$x^2 + (x - 10)^2 = (50)^2$$
$$x^2 + x^2 - 20x + 100 = 2{,}500$$
$$2x^2 - 20x - 2{,}400 = 0$$
$$2(x^2 - 10x - 1{,}200) = 0$$
$$2(x - 40)(x + 30) = 0$$
$$x = 40 \quad x = -30$$

Since x represents a distance, it cannot be –30, so $x = 40$. Juan walks a total of $(40 - 10) + 40 =$ 70 m to get to the park.

36. C: The expression representing the monthly charge for Company A is $\$25 + \$0.05m$, where m is the time in minutes spent talking on the phone. Set this expression equal to the monthly charge for Company B, which is \$50. Solve for m to find the number of minutes the two companies charge the same amount.

$$\$25 + \$0.05m = \$50$$
$$\$0.05m = \$25$$
$$m = 500$$

Notice that the answer choices are given in hours, not in minutes. Since there are 60 minutes in an hour, $m = \frac{500}{60}$ hours $= 8\frac{1}{3}$ hours. One-third of an hour is 20 minutes, so m is 8 hours and 20 minutes.

37. C: When the dress is marked down by 20%, the cost of the dress is 80% of its original price. Since a percentage can be written as a fraction by placing the percentage over 100, the reduced price of the dress can be written as $\frac{80}{100}x$, or $\frac{4}{5}x$, where x is the original price. When discounted an extra 25%, the dress costs 75% of the reduced price. This results in the expression $\frac{75}{100}\left(\frac{4}{5}x\right)$, which can be simplified to $\frac{3}{4}\left(\frac{4}{5}x\right)$, or $\frac{3}{5}x$. So the final price of the dress is three-fifths of the original price.

38. A: Since rate in mph $= \frac{\text{distance in miles}}{\text{time in hours}}$, Oliver's speed on the way to the park and back home in mph can be expressed as $\frac{d}{0.5}$ and $\frac{d}{1.5}$, respectively, when d is the distance between Oliver's house and his destination. Since he went 4 mph slower on his way home, $\frac{d}{0.5} - \frac{d}{1.5} = 4$, or $\frac{2d}{1} - \frac{2d}{3} = 4$.

$$3\left(2d - \frac{2d}{3}\right) = (4)3$$
$$6d - 2d = 12$$
$$d = 3$$

Since the distance between Oliver's house and the park is 3 miles, he traveled a total distance of 6 miles in two hours. Therefore, his average speed was $\frac{6\text{ miles}}{2\text{ hours}} = 3$ mph.

39. B: In choice A, the teacher surveys all the members of the population in which he is interested. However, since the response is voluntary, the survey is biased. The participants are self-selected rather than randomly selected. It may be that students who have a strong opinion are more likely to respond than those who are more neutral, and this would give the teacher a skewed perspective of student opinions. In choice B, students are randomly selected, so the sampling technique is not biased. In choice C, the student uses convenience sampling, which is a biased technique. For example, perhaps the student is in an honors class; his sampling method would not be representative of the entire class of eleventh graders, which includes both students who take and who do not take honors classes. Choice D also represents convenience sampling; only the opinions of parents in the PTA are examined, and these parents' opinions may not reflect the opinions of all parents of students at the school.

40. B: To find the integral, use u-substitution. Since the derivative and integral of e^x is itself but this function has e raised to a power, use the power as u when doing u-substitution.

$$\int 3x^2 e^{x^3}\,dx \qquad \text{Let } u = x^3;\ du = 3x^2 dx$$

$$\int e^u\,du = e^u + C$$

$$= e^{x^3} + C$$

41. B: The heterozygous combinations that include b are ab, ba, bc, and cb. We add these and divide by 250 to find the probability that a person in this group has one of the above combinations.

$$\frac{8 + 10 + 52 + 32}{250} = \frac{102}{250} = 0.408$$

Multiply this experimental probability by 50,000 to find the number of individuals expected to be heterozygous for the b allele in a population of 50,000.

$$0.408 \times 50{,}000 = 20{,}400$$

Therefore, 20,400 individuals will be heterozygous for the b allele.

42. C: Ava and Jack hiked 8 miles from home and then back again, so they traveled a total of 16 miles. Therefore, statement III is true. They traveled these 16 miles in 7 hours, so their average speed was $\frac{16}{7}$ mph or approximately 2.3 mph. Therefore, statement I is false. Ava and Jack hiked 2 miles from point B to C in 1 hour, so they were hiking at a speed of 2 mph. They hiked 6 miles from D to E in 3 hours, so they hiked $\frac{6\text{ miles}}{3\text{ hours}} = \frac{2\text{ miles}}{1\text{ hour}} = 2$ mph. Therefore, their speed was the same during both these times, and statement II is also true.

43. A: Since all of the answer choices are parallelograms, determine whether the parallelogram is also a rhombus or a rectangle or a square. One way to do this is by examining the parallelogram's diagonals. If the parallelogram's diagonals are perpendicular, then the parallelogram is a rhombus. If the parallelogram's diagonals are congruent, then the parallelogram is a rectangle. If a parallelogram is both a rhombus and a rectangle, then it is a square. To determine whether the diagonals are perpendicular, find the slopes of the diagonals of the quadrilateral.

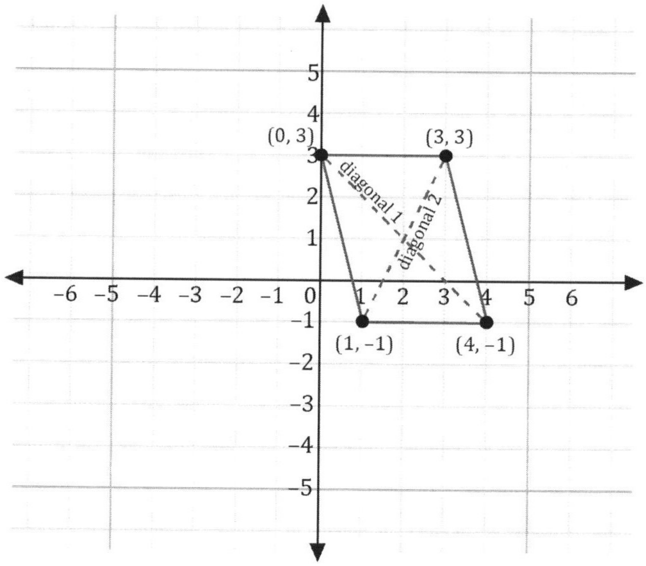

Diagonal 1

$$\frac{-1-3}{4-0} = \frac{-4}{4} = -1$$

Diagonal 2

$$\frac{3-(-1)}{3-1} = \frac{4}{2} = 2$$

The diagonals do not have opposite reciprocal slopes, so they are not perpendicular. Thus, the parallelogram is *not* a rhombus or a square. To determine whether the diagonals are congruent, find the lengths of the diagonals of the quadrilateral:

Diagonal 1

$$\begin{aligned}\sqrt{(4-0)^2+(-1-3)^2} &= \sqrt{(4)^2+(-4)^2}\\ &= \sqrt{16+16}\\ &= \sqrt{32}\end{aligned}$$

Diagonal 2

$$\begin{aligned}\sqrt{(3-1)^2+(3-(-1))^2} &= \sqrt{(2)^2+(4)^2}\\ &= \sqrt{4+16}\\ &= \sqrt{20}\end{aligned}$$

The diagonals are not congruent, so the parallelogram is not a rectangle. The polygon must be a parallelogram.

44. B: First, use the properties of logarithms to solve for y:

$3\log_3 y + \log_3 3 = 4$	Write out the equation given.
$\log_3 y^3 + \log_3 3 = 4$	Rewrite the first term using the power rule of logarithms: $p \cdot \log_b m = \log_b m^p$.
$\log_3 3y^3 = 4$	Rewrite the left side using the product rule of logarithms: $\log_b m + \log_b n = \log_b mn$.
$3y^3 = 3^4$	Rewrite the logarithmic equation as an exponential equation.
$3y^3 = 81$	Simplify the right side.
$y^3 = 27$	Divide both sides by 3.
$y = 3$	Take the cube root of both sides.

Finally, substitute 3 for y in the expression $\log_y 243$ and simplify: $\log_3 243 = 5$ since $3^5 = 243$.

45. D: ΔABC is similar to the smaller triangle with which it shares vertex B.

$$AB = (2x + 1) + (x + 2) = 3x + 3$$
$$BC = 4 + 6 = 10$$

Set up a proportion and solve for x.

$$\frac{3x + 3}{10} = \frac{x + 2}{4}$$
$$4(3x + 3) = 10(x + 2)$$
$$12x + 12 = 10x + 20$$
$$2x = 8$$
$$x = 4$$

So, $AB = 3x + 3 = 3(4) + 3 = 15$.

46. B: The Babylonians used a base-60 numeral system, which is still used in the division of an hour into 60 minutes, a minute into 60 seconds, and a circle into 360 degrees. The word "algebra" and its development as a discipline separate from geometry are attributed to the Arabic/Islamic civilization. The Greek philosopher Thales is credited with using deductive reasoning to prove geometric concepts. Boolean logic was introduced by British mathematician George Boole.

47. A: A system of linear equations can be solved by using matrices or by using the graphing, substitution, or elimination method. The elimination method is shown here.

$$\begin{cases} 3x + y = 1 \\ -4x + 3y = 29 \end{cases}$$

To eliminate y by the elimination method, multiply the top equation by –3 so that the coefficients of the y-terms will be additive inverses.

$$-3(3x + y) = (1)(-3)$$
$$-9x - 3y = -3$$

Then, add the two equations and solve for x.

$$\begin{array}{rrrcr} & -9x & -3y & = & -3 \\ + & -4x & +3y & = & 29 \\ \hline & & -13x & = & 26 \\ & & x & = & -2 \end{array}$$

Substitute –2 for x in either of the given equations and solve for y. Here $x = -2$ is substituted into the top equation.

$$3(-2) + y = 1$$
$$-6 + y = 1$$
$$y = 7$$

The solution to the system of equations is $(-2, 7)$.

48. B: Use the table of values to first write equations for $f(x)$ and $g(x)$: $f(x) = 2x^3$ and $g(x) = 3x - 5$. Then, use those equations to find $f(g(3))$.

$$g(3) = 3(3) - 5 = 9 - 5 = 4$$
$$f(4) = 2(4)^3 = 2(64) = 128$$

So, $f\left(g(3)\right) = f(4) = 128$.

49. B: All regular polygons have rotational symmetry. The angle of rotation is the smallest angle by which the polygon can be rotated such that it maps onto itself; any multiple of this angle will also map the polygon onto itself. The angle of rotation for a regular polygon is the angle formed between two lines drawn from consecutive vertices to the center of the polygon. Since the vertices of a regular polygon lie on a circle, for a regular polygon with n sides, the angle of rotation measures $\frac{360°}{n}$. Therefore, a square has rotational symmetry about the angle 90° and its multiples. A regular hexagon has rotational symmetry about the angle 60° and its multiples. A regular octagon has rotational symmetry about 45° and its multiples. And a regular decagon has rotational symmetry about 36° and its multiples. Since 120° is a multiple of 60°, the correct answer is a regular hexagon.

50. C: The two functions that combine to form $g(x)$ meet at $x = 2$. The slope is positive to the left of $x = 2$, rising to the intersection point (2,2). The slope is negative to the right of $x = 2$. Thus, while the domain of $g(x)$ is all real numbers because there is an output for every possible x-value, the range is $y \leq 2$. We can find the solution when $x = 1$ by plugging 1 into the bottom equation, since 1 is less than 2. If $g(x) = x$ and $x = 1$, then $g(1) = 1$. So, statements I and II are true, while statement III is false.

51. A: First, set the equation equal to zero, then factor it.

$$3x^3y^2 - 45x^2y = 15x^3y - 9x^2y^2$$
$$3x^3y^2 - 15x^3y + 9x^2y^2 - 45x^2y = 0$$
$$3x^2y(xy - 5x + 3y - 15) = 0$$
$$3x^2y[x(y-5) + 3(y-5)] = 0$$
$$3x^2y[(y-5)(x+3)] = 0$$

Use the zero product property to find the solutions.

$$3x^2y = 0 \qquad y - 5 = 0 \qquad x + 3 = 0$$
$$x = 0 \qquad y = 5 \qquad x = -3$$
$$y = 0$$

So, the solutions are $x = \{0, -3\}$ and $y = \{0,5\}$.

52. C: Multiply the second equation by 2 and combine it with the first equation to eliminate y.

$$\begin{array}{rrrrcr} & 2x & -4y & +1z & = & 10 \\ + & -6x & +4y & -8z & = & -14 \\ \hline & -4x & & -7z & = & -4 \end{array}$$

Multiply the third equation by –2 and combine it with the original second equation to eliminate y.

$$\begin{array}{rrrrcr} & -3x & +2y & -4z & = & -7 \\ + & -2x & -2y & +6z & = & 2 \\ \hline & -5x & & +2z & = & -5 \end{array}$$

Multiply the equation from step one by 5 and the equation from step two by –4 and combine to eliminate x.

$$\begin{array}{rrrcr} & -20x & -35z & = & -20 \\ + & 20x & -\ 8z & = & 20 \\ \hline & & -43z & = & 0 \\ & & z & = & 0 \end{array}$$

Substitute 0 for z in the equation from step 2 to find x.

$$-5x + 2(0) = -5$$
$$-5x = -5$$
$$x = 1$$

Substitute 0 for z and 1 for x into the first original equation to find y.

$$2(1) - 4y + (0) = 10$$
$$2 - 4y = 10$$
$$-4y = 8$$
$$y = -2$$

Therefore, the solution to the system of equations is $(1, -2, 0)$.

53. D: The symbol $\wedge$ is the logical conjunction symbol. In order for statement $(p \wedge q)$ to be true, both statements p and q must be true. The $\neg$ symbol means "not," so if $(p \wedge q)$ is true, then $\neg(p \wedge q)$ is false, and if $(p \wedge q)$ is false, then $\neg(p \wedge q)$ is true. The statement $q \leftrightarrow \neg(p \wedge q)$ is true when the value of q is the same as the value of $\neg(p \wedge q)$.

p	q	$(p \wedge q)$	$\neg(p \wedge q)$	$q \leftrightarrow \neg(p \wedge q)$
T	T	T	F	F
T	F	F	T	F
F	T	F	T	T
F	F	F	T	F

54. B: The average number of females per age bracket is the total number of females divided by 4, or $\frac{297}{4} = 74.25$. The number of volunteers at the animal shelter is 13% of the total number of volunteers (626), which is $0.13(626) = 81.38$. The difference in the number of male and female volunteers is $329 - 297 = 32$, and the difference in the number of people over 60 and people under 21 is $187 - 118 = 69$. The greatest quantity of the answer choices is the number of volunteers at the animal shelter.

55. C: 65 of 118 volunteers under the age of 21 are male. So, the probability that a male is chosen is $\frac{\text{number of 0–20 year–old males}}{\text{number of 0–20 year–olds}} = \frac{65}{118} \approx 0.55$.

56. C: A rectangular prism has six rectangular faces. The arrangement of these faces in a two-dimensional figure is a net of a rectangular prism if the figure can be folded to form a rectangular prism. Choices A, B, and D represent three of the possible nets of a rectangular prism (note that choice D is a cube, which is a type of rectangular prism). Choice C is not a viable net.

57. A: The recursive definition gives the first term of the sequence, $a_1 = -1$. Each term afterward is the sum of the previous term and 2. So the second term is $-1 + 2 = 1$, the third term is $1 + 2 = 3$, and so on.

n	a_n
1	-1
2	1
3	3

The relationship between n and a_n is linear, so the equation of the sequence can be found in the same way as the equation of a line. The value of a_n increases by 2 each time the value of n increases by 1.

n	$2n$	a_n
1	2	-1
2	4	1
3	6	3

Since the difference between $2n$ and a_n is 3, $a_n = 2n - 3$.

n	$2n - 3$	a_n
1	$2 - 3 = -1$	-1
2	$4 - 3 = 1$	1
3	$6 - 3 = 3$	3

58. C: There are $(n - 1)!$ ways to arrange n units around a circle for $n > 1$. So, for 7 people in a circle, there are 6! distinguishable seating arrangements.

$$(n - 1)! = (7 - 1)! = 6! = 720$$

Therefore, there are 720 distinguishable ways a group of 7 can be seated at a circular table.

59. D: "The square of three times the sum of a and six is fourteen more than a" is represented by the equation $[3(a + 6)]^2 = a + 14$. Solve for a.

$$\begin{aligned} [3a + 18]^2 &= a + 14 \\ 9a^2 + 108a + 324 &= a + 14 \\ 9a^2 + 107a + 310 &= 0 \\ (a + 5)(9a + 62) &= 0 \\ a &= -5, -\frac{62}{9} \end{aligned}$$

So, –5 is a possible value of a.

60. C: Bacterial growth is exponential. Let x be the number of doubling times, let a be the number of bacteria in the colony originally, and let y be the number of bacteria after x doubling times. After 2 hours, the population would have doubled four times:

$$\begin{aligned} a(2^4) &= 6 \times 10^5 \\ 16a &= 6 \times 10^5 \\ a &= 3.75 \times 10^4 \end{aligned}$$

The equation for determining the number of bacteria is $y = (2^x)(3.75 \times 10^4)$. Since the bacteria double every 30 minutes, they go through two doubling times every hour. So, when the bacteria are allowed to grow for 10 hours, they will have gone through 20 doubling times. When $x = 20$, $y = (2^{20})(3.75 \times 10^4) = 3{,}932{,}160 \times 10^4$, which is approximately 3.9×10^{10}.

61. C: The distance that is being traveled and the speed are known. If we let the number of hours the trip will take be x, then we can solve the problem in the following way:

$$\begin{aligned} distance &= speed \times time \\ 827 \text{ km} &= 64 \, \frac{\text{km}}{\text{hr}} \times x \\ \frac{827 \text{ km}}{64 \, \frac{\text{km}}{\text{hr}}} &= x \\ 12.92 \text{ hours} &= x \end{aligned}$$

Rounding off, we get 13 hours.

62. C: We can find the area of the white part by viewing the target as five separate circles of various sizes, one inside the other. We ignore the outer circle since we are only interested in the white parts, and add the areas of the two white circles and subtract the areas of the two interior shaded circles. The formula for area of a circle is πr^2, so the area of the largest white circle is $\pi(8m)^2$. We subtract the shaded circle inside it, add the white circle inside that one, and then subtract the smallest shaded circle.

$$\begin{aligned} A &= \pi(8m)^2 - \pi(6m)^2 + \pi(4m)^2 - \pi(2m)^2 \\ &= 64\pi m^2 - 36\pi m^2 + 16\pi m^2 - 4\pi m^2 \\ &= (64 - 36 + 16 - 4)\pi m^2 \\ &= 40\pi m^2 \end{aligned}$$

63. A: Use a Venn diagram to help organize the given information. Start by filling in the space where the three circles intersect: one student enrolled in all three areas. Use that information to fill in the spaces where two circles intersect. For example, seven students are taking both Intro to Law and Latin, and one of those is also taking Biophysics, so six students are taking Intro to Law and Latin but not Biophysics. Once the diagram is completed, add the number of students from each portion of the diagram. The total number of students taking special electives is $12 + 14 + 9 + 3 + 1 + 6 + 1 = 46$.

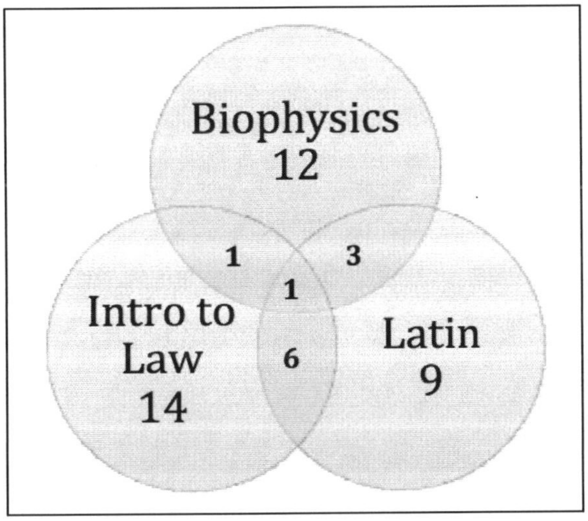

64. D: Since a and b are multiples of 6, each can be expressed as the product of 6 and an integer. So, if we write $a = 6x$ and $b = 6y$ then, $3(6x)^2 + 2(6y)^3 = c$. Simplify and factor.

$$3(6x)^2 + 2(6y)^3 = c$$
$$108x^2 + 432y^3 = c$$
$$108(x^2 + 4y^3) = c$$

Since c is the product of 108 and some other integer, 108 must be a factor of c.

65. C: A quick estimation of the number of feet the mountain climber climbs is found by rounding each day's climb to the nearest hundred feet and finding the sum. 480 rounds to 500, 610 rounds to 600, 295 rounds to 300, and 303 also rounds to 300.

$$500 + 600 + 300 + 300 = 1{,}700$$

Therefore, she climbed approximately 1,700 feet.

66. B: The area of a triangle is $A = \frac{1}{2}bh$, where b and h are the lengths of the triangle's base and height, respectively. The base of the given triangle is x, but the height is not given. Since the triangle is a right triangle and the hypotenuse is given, the triangle's height can be found using the Pythagorean theorem.

$$x^2 + h^2 = 6^2$$
$$h = \sqrt{36 - x^2}$$

To find the area of the triangle in terms of x, substitute $\sqrt{36 - x^2}$ for the height and x for the base of the triangle into the area formula $\left(A = \frac{1}{2}bh\right)$:

$$A(x) = \frac{1}{2}(x)(\sqrt{36 - x^2})$$

$$A(x) = \frac{x\sqrt{36 - x^2}}{2}$$

67. A: Get as many terms as possible out from the radical and any radicals out from the denominator. First, identify perfect squares under the radical.

$$\sqrt{\frac{-28x^6}{27y^5}} = \sqrt{\frac{-4x^6 \times (7)}{9y^4 \times (3y)}} = \sqrt{\frac{-(2x^3)^2 \times (7)}{(3y^2)^2 \times (3y)}}$$

Then, pull out the perfect squares from under the radical.

$$\frac{2x^3 i\sqrt{7}}{3y^2\sqrt{3y}}$$

Finally, rationalize the denominator.

$$\frac{2x^3 i\sqrt{7}}{3y^2\sqrt{3y}} \times \frac{\sqrt{3y}}{\sqrt{3y}} = \frac{2x^3 i\sqrt{21y}}{9y^3}$$

Therefore, the simplified expression is $\frac{2x^3 i\sqrt{21y}}{9y^3}$.

68. A: The length rounded to the nearest hundred centimeters is 1,300 cm. The width rounded to the nearest hundred centimeters is 700 cm. The area of the rectangle is the product of the length and the width or $1300 \times 700 = 910{,}000 \text{ cm}^2$.

69. C: The graph shown is the exponential function $y = 2^x$. Notice that the graph passes through (0,1) and (2,4). A quick check of each option can be done to eliminate answer choices.

x	x^2	$\sqrt{x}$	2^x	$\log_2 x$
0	0	0	1	undefined
2	4	$\sqrt{2}$	4	1

70. B: The side lengths rounded to the nearest ten centimeters are 20 cm, 20 cm, and 10 cm. Then the estimated perimeter is the sum found by adding $20 + 20 + 10 = 50$. The perimeter is about 50 cm.

71. A: One way to find an inverse function is to take the original equation describing the function, replace $f(x)$ with x and x with $f^{-1}(x)$, and then solve for $f^{-1}(x)$. In this case, $f(x) = \tan(2x + 4)$ becomes $x = \tan(2f^{-1}(x) + 4)$. To solve for $f^{-1}(x)$, first take the inverse tangent of both sides: $\tan^{-1} x = \tan^{-1}(\tan(2f^{-1}(x) + 4)) = 2f^{-1}(x) + 4$. Now subtract four from both sides: $\tan^{-1} x - 4 = 2f^{-1}(x)$. Finally, divide both sides by 2: $\frac{1}{2}(\tan^{-1} x - 4) = f^{-1}(x)$, or $f^{-1}(x) = \frac{1}{2}\tan^{-1} x - 2$.

72. B: Determine the probability of each option.

For choice A, this is the total number of students in the tea circle of the Venn diagram divided by the total number of students surveyed:

$$\frac{42 + 12 + 7 + 26}{250} = \frac{87}{250} = 34.8\%$$

For choice B, this is the total number of students in the hot chocolate circle and in at least one other circle divided by the total number in the hot chocolate circle:

$$\frac{31 + 7 + 26}{31 + 7 + 26 + 56} = \frac{64}{120} \approx 53.3\%$$

For choice C, this is the number of students in the intersection of all three circles divided by the total number in the overlap of the coffee and hot chocolate circles:

$$\frac{7}{7 + 31} = \frac{7}{38} \approx 18.4\%$$

For choice D, this is the number of students outside of all the circles divided by the total number of students surveyed:

$$\frac{11}{250} = 4.4\%$$

Choice B has the greatest probability.

73. D: See the pattern from the table.

Years after purchase	0	1	2	3
Number of llamas	32	48	72	108

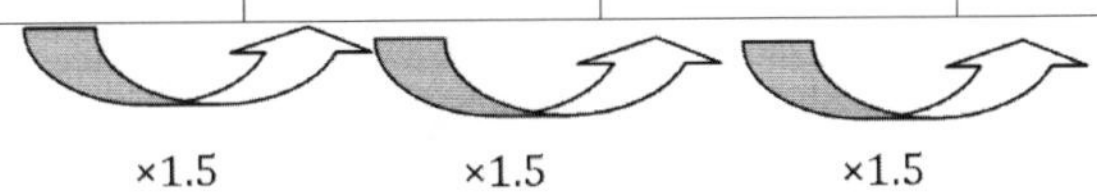

Multiplying 108 by 1.5 gives the predicted value 4 years after purchase $108 \times 1.5 = 162$.

74. D: First, add the two straight 150-yard portions. Also, note that the distance for the two semi-circles put together is the circumference of a circle. Since the circumference of a circle is π times the diameter, the length of the circular portion of the track is simply 30π. Then, add this to the length of the two straight portions of the track.

$$\text{Perimeter} = 30\pi + (2 \times 150) \approx 394.25$$

Therefore, the perimeter of the entire track is approximately 395 yards.

75. B: The center of the sphere is shared by the center of the cube, and each of the corners of the cube touches the surface of the sphere. Therefore, the diameter of the sphere is the line that passes through the center of the cube and connects one corner of the cube to the opposite corner on the opposite face. Notice in the illustration below that the diameter d of the sphere can be represented as the hypotenuse of a right triangle with a short leg measuring 5 units. Since the volume of the cube is 125 cubic units, each of its sides measure $\sqrt[3]{125} = 5$ units. The long leg of the triangle is the diagonal of the base of the cube. Its length can be found using the Pythagorean theorem:

$$5^2 + 5^2 = x^2$$
$$x = \sqrt{50} = 5\sqrt{2}$$

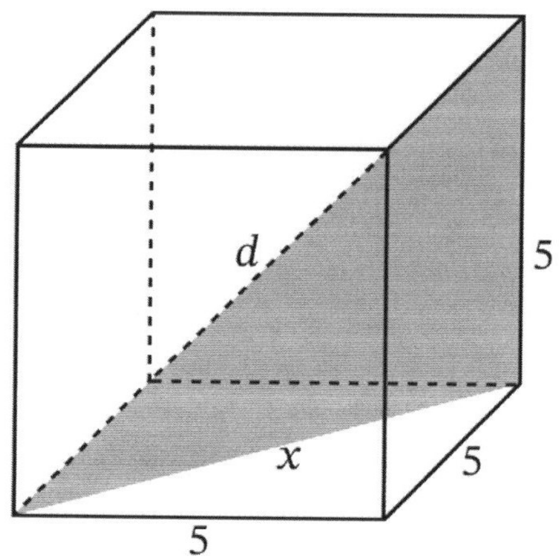

Use the Pythagorean theorem again to find d, the diameter of the sphere: $d^2 = \left(5\sqrt{2}\right)^2 + 5^2$, which then becomes $d = \sqrt{75} = 5\sqrt{3}$.

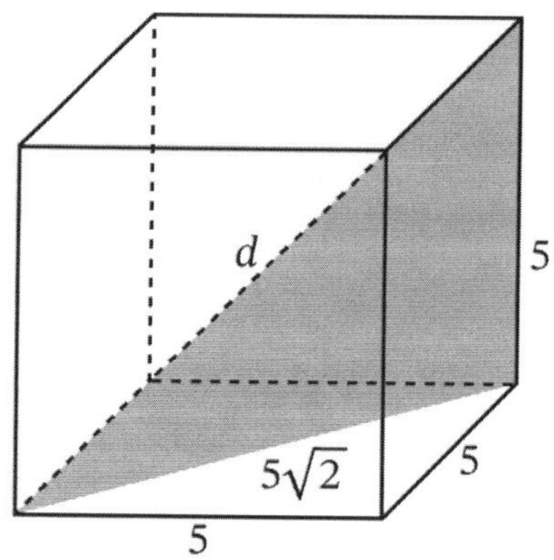

To find the volume of the sphere, use the formula $V = \frac{4}{3}\pi r^3$. Since the radius r of the sphere is half the diameter, $r = \frac{5\sqrt{3}}{2}$, and $V = \frac{4}{3}\pi\left(\frac{5\sqrt{3}}{2}\right)^3 = \frac{4}{3}\pi\left(\frac{375\sqrt{3}}{8}\right) = \frac{125\pi\sqrt{3}}{2}$ cubic units.

76. B: If l and w represent the length and width of the enclosed area, its perimeter is equal to $2l + 2w$. The fence is positioned x feet from the lot's edges on each side, so the perimeter of the enlarged garden is $2(l + 2x) + 2(w + 2x)$. The extra amount of money spent by fencing the larger area is \$36, and since the fencing material costs \$1.50 per linear foot, 24 more feet of material are used to fence around the garden than would have been used for the original. This can be expressed as the equation:

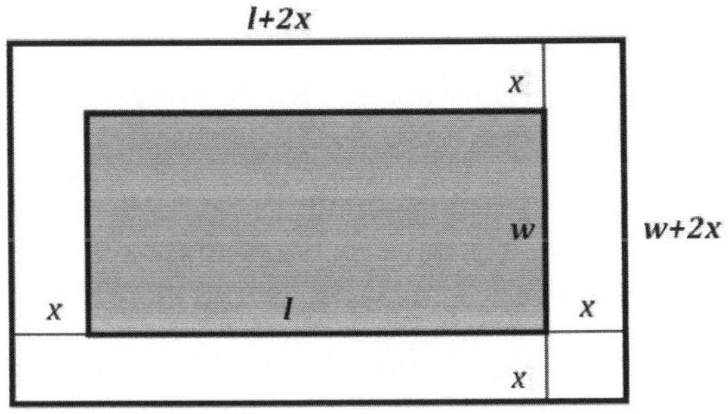

$$\begin{aligned} 2(l+2x)+2(w+2x)-(2l+2w) &= 24 \\ 2l+4x+2w+4x-2l-2w &= 24 \\ 8x &= 24 \\ x &= 3 \end{aligned}$$

This means that Marcus moved the boundary line back 3 feet on each of the four sides. The difference in the area of the lot and the enclosed space is 34 yd^2, which is the same as 306 ft^2. So, $(l+2x)(w+2x)-lw=306$. Substituting 3 for x, we get the following equation and solve.

$$\begin{aligned} (l+6)(w+6)-lw &= 306 \\ lw+6l+6w+36-lw &= 306 \\ 6l+6w &= 270 \\ 6(l+w) &= 270 \\ l+w &= 45 \end{aligned}$$

Therefore, the length plus the width is equal to 45 feet. This is the original length and width, so we add 6 to each, or 12 total, for a new length and width of 57 feet. Therefore, the perimeter of the enclosed space, $2(l+w)$, is $2(57)=114$ ft. The cost of 114 ft of chicken wire is $114 \times \$1.50 = \$171$.

77. C: Since there are 100 cm in a meter, on a 1: 150 scale drawing, each centimeter represents 1.5 m. Therefore, an area of one square centimeter on the drawing represents 2.25 square meters in the real room. Since the area of the room in the scale drawing is 20 cm^2, the room's actual area is 45 m^2.

Another way to determine the area of the room is to write and solve an equation using the area formula for a rectangle.

$\frac{l}{150} \times \frac{w}{150} = 20\text{ cm}^2$, where l and w are the dimensions of the actual room:

$$\frac{lw}{22{,}500} = 20\text{ cm}^2$$

$$\text{Area} = 450{,}000\text{ cm}^2$$

Since this is not one of the answer choices, convert cm^2 to m^2:

$$450{,}000\text{ cm}^2 \times \frac{1\text{ m}}{100\text{ cm}} \times \frac{1\text{ m}}{100\text{ cm}} = 45\text{ m}^2$$

78. A: The given values make the Pythagorean theorem true, that is $5^2+12^2=13^2$. So, this is a right triangle. Let the base of the triangle be $5x$ and the height of the triangle be $12x$. So, the area is $A=\frac{1}{2}bh$, or $\frac{1}{2}(5x)(12x)=30x^2$.

79. D: Since a and b are even integers, each can be expressed as the product of 2 and an integer. So, if we let $a = 2x$ and $b = 2y$, then $3(2x)^2 + 9(2y)^3 = c$.

$$3(4x^2) + 9(8y^3) = c$$
$$12x^2 + 72y^3 = c$$
$$12(x^2 + 6y^3) = c$$

Since c is the product of 12 and some other integer, 12 must be a factor of c. Incidentally, the numbers 2, 3, and 6 must also be factors of c since each is also a factor of 12.

80. A: 25% of the data in a set is above the third quartile. Since the third quartile for this set is 86, there is a 25% chance that a student chosen at random from Math scored above an 86.

81. B: The line through the center of the box represents the median. The median test score for English and History is the same, not the mean test score, which makes choice B the correct answer. Note that for Science, the median is a better representation of the data than the mean. There is at least one outlier (a point that lies outside of two standard deviations from the mean), which brings down the average test score. In cases such as this, the mean is not the best measure of central tendency, so choice A is not the correct answer. The median of the History scores is 87, and the 3rd quartile scores for Math is also 87, so choice C is not the answer. The median of the English scores is 86, and based on the spread of data, the mean is lower than the median, so choice D is also not correct.

82. B: First, square the binomial.

$$(3 - 2i)^2 + (7 + 7i) = 9 - 12i + 4i^2 + 7 + 7i$$

Then, simplify $i^2 = -1$.

$$9 - 12i - 4 + 7 + 7i$$

Finally, combine like terms.

$$12 - 5i$$

83. B: On the unit circle, $\sin\theta = \frac{\sqrt{2}}{2}$ when $\theta = \frac{\pi}{4}$ and when $\theta = \frac{3\pi}{4}$. Only $\frac{3\pi}{4}$ fits the condition $\frac{\pi}{2} < \theta < \pi$, so $\theta = \frac{3\pi}{4}$.

84. A: Pythagoras made many important contributions to the field of mathematics. One such contribution, the Pythagorean formula $a^2 + b^2 = c^2$, can be used to solve for the legs or hypotenuse of a right triangle.

85. D: Since the midterm has a low outlier, this skews and decreases the mean for the data set. Therefore, it is not the best reflection of student performance at the midterm. The median would be more accurate. The line in the middle of the box represents the median of the data set, so the median for assessment 2 and the final is the same, not necessarily the mean. Looking at the middle lines of the four boxes, the highest median grades happened with assessment 2 and the final. Since there is a high outlier for assessment 2, this skews the mean higher, meaning it will be greater than the median for this test. Therefore, choice D is correct.

86. A: If $y = -a(x+b)(x+c)^2$, the degree of the polynomial is 3. Since the degree of the polynomial is odd and the leading coefficient is negative ($a < 0$), the end behavior of the graph goes to $(\infty, -\infty)$ and $(-\infty, \infty)$. Therefore, only Choice A is a possible graph of this function.

87. B: The inequality is solved by writing a double inequality equivalent to the given inequality but without the absolute value bars.

$$-9 < x + 6 < 9$$

Solve the double inequality by subtracting 6 from all three parts.

$$-15 < x < 3$$

The solution set can be written using interval notation.

$$(-15,3)$$

88. C: In a parallelogram, consecutive angles are supplementary; that is, the sum of their measures is 180°. Use this to write an equation and then solve for x.

$$\begin{aligned} \text{m}\angle A + \text{m}\angle B &= 180^\circ \\ (5x) + (2x - 9) &= 180 \\ 7x - 9 &= 180 \\ 7x &= 189 \\ x &= 27 \end{aligned}$$

In a parallelogram, opposite angles are congruent. Thus, $\text{m}\angle B = \text{m}\angle C$, so find the value of $\text{m}\angle B$.

$$\begin{aligned} \text{m}\angle B &= 2x - 9 \\ &= 2(27) - 9 \\ &= 45^\circ \end{aligned}$$

Therefore, $\text{m}\angle C = 45^\circ$.

89. C: The recursive definition of the sequence gives the first term of the series, $a_1 = -2$. The definition also defines each term in the series as the sum of the previous term and $\frac{1}{2}$. Therefore, the second term in the series is $-2 + \frac{1}{2} = -\frac{3}{2}$, the third term in the series is $-\frac{3}{2} + \frac{1}{2} = -1$, and so on.

n	a_n
1	-2
2	$-\frac{3}{2}$
3	-1

The relationship between n and a_n is linear, so the equation of the sequence can be found in the same way as the equation of a line. The value of a_n increases by $\frac{1}{2}$ each time the value of n increases by 1.

n	$\frac{n}{2}$	a_n
1	$\frac{1}{2}$	-2
2	1	$-\frac{3}{2}$
3	$\frac{3}{2}$	-1

Since the difference between $\frac{1}{2}n$ and a_n is $-\frac{5}{2}$. So, $a_n = \frac{1}{2}n - \frac{5}{2}$.

n	$\frac{n}{2} - \frac{5}{2}$	a_n
1	$\frac{1}{2} - \frac{5}{2}$	-2
2	$1 - \frac{5}{2}$	$-\frac{3}{2}$
3	$\frac{3}{2} - \frac{5}{2}$	-1

90. D: There are many ways Josephine may have applied her knowledge to determine how to approximately measure her medicine using her plastic spoon. The expression below shows how she converts from cubic centimeters to spoons.

$$25 \text{ cc} \times \frac{1 \text{ mL}}{1 \text{ cc}} \times \frac{1\text{L}}{1{,}000 \text{ mL}} \times \frac{0.5 \text{ gal}}{2 \text{ L}} \times \frac{16 \text{ c}}{1 \text{ gal}} \times \frac{48 \text{ t}}{1 \text{ c}} \times \frac{1 \text{ spoonful}}{1 \text{ t}}$$

$$\frac{25}{1{,}000} \times \frac{1}{4} \times 16 \times 48$$

The only choice which correctly uses dimensional analysis is choice D.

91. C: There are seven musical notes A–G, so this would not work for eight students.

92. D: If x is a positive, even integer and the greatest common factor of x and y is greater than 1, the greatest common factor of x and y must be at least as great as y. For example, if x is 2 and y is 4, the greatest common factor is 2 and the least common multiple is 4, which is equal to y. Or if x is 6 and y is 9, the greatest common factor is 3 and the least common multiple is 18, which is greater than y.

93. D: If each of the 5 groups will contain 4 boys and 4 girls, there must be 20 boys and 20 girls in the class. Since the order of the boys and girls does not matter in the group, the situation represents a combination. The number of ways to select 4 individuals from a group of 20 is:

$$_{20}C_4 = \frac{20!}{4!\,(20-4)!} = \frac{20!}{4!\,16!} = \frac{20 \times 19 \times 18 \times 17 \times 16!}{4!\,16!} = \frac{20 \times 19 \times 18 \times 17}{4 \times 3 \times 2 \times 1} = 4{,}845$$

This value is the same for the boys and the girls. Since each combination of boys can be paired with each combination of girls, the number of group combinations is $4{,}845 \times 4{,}845 = 23{,}474{,}025$.

94. B: If each number is rounded to the nearest thousand, 15,012 rounds to 15,000, and 19,938 rounds to 20,000. We would therefore expect $\frac{15{,}012}{19{,}938}$ to be close to $\frac{15{,}000}{20{,}000}$, which can be simplified to $\frac{15{,}000 \div 1{,}000}{20{,}000 \div 1{,}000} = \frac{15}{20} = \frac{15 \div 5}{20 \div 5} = \frac{3}{4}$.

95. B: The sine function is represented by the ratio $\frac{\text{opposite leg}}{\text{hypotenuse}}$. So, the sine of angle A can be written as $\frac{BC}{AB}$. The cosine function is represented by the ratio $\frac{\text{adjacent leg}}{\text{hypotenuse}}$. In ΔABC, $\cos B$ can also be written as $\frac{BC}{AB}$. We can also determine that angle B is 62°. Since the two acute angles of a right triangle are complementary, we can find that angle A is $90 - 62 = 28°$. Since we can see that the sine of angle A is equal to the cosine of angle B, we know that the cosine of angle A will also be equal to the sine of angle B. So $\cos A = \sin B = \sin 62°$.

96. C: If all possible outcomes are equally likely, then the probability of an event is the number of outcomes in which that event occurs, divided by the number of possible outcomes. A camper who is at least eight years old can be eight, nine, or ten years old, so the probability of randomly selecting a camper at least eight years old is:

$$\frac{\text{number of eight-, nine-, and ten-year-old campers}}{\text{total number of campers}} = \frac{14 + 12 + 10}{12 + 15 + 14 + 12 + 10} = \frac{36}{63} = \frac{4}{7}$$

97. D: A score of 85 is one standard deviation below the mean. Since approximately 68% of the data is within one standard deviation of the mean, about 32% (100% − 68%) of the data is outside of one standard deviation within the mean. Normally distributed data is symmetric about the mean, which means that about 16% of the data lies below one standard deviation below the mean and about 16% of data lies above one standard deviation above the mean. Therefore, approximately 16% of individuals have IQs less than 85, while approximately 84% of the population has an IQ of at least 85. Since 84% of 300 is 252, about 252 people from the selected group have IQs of at least 85.

98. B: First, apply the laws of exponents to simplify the expression on the left. Then, find a common denominator to add the fractions.

$\frac{(x^2y)(2xy^{-2})^3}{16x^5y^2} + \frac{3}{xy}$	
$\frac{(x^2y)(8x^3y^{-6})}{16x^5y^2} + \frac{3}{xy}$	Simplify the second term in the left numerator using the exponent rule $(x^m)^n = x^{m \cdot n}$.
$\frac{8x^5y^{-5}}{16x^5y^2} + \frac{3}{xy}$	Simplify the numerator of the left fraction using the exponent rule $x^m \cdot x^n = x^{m+n}$.
$\frac{1}{2y^7} + \frac{3}{xy}$	Simplify the left fraction using the exponent rule $\frac{x^m}{x^n} = x^{m-n}$.

$\frac{1}{2y^7} \cdot \frac{x}{x} + \frac{3}{xy} \cdot \frac{2y^6}{2y^6}$	Create common denominators between the two fractions.
$\frac{x}{2xy^7} + \frac{6y^6}{2xy^7}$	Simplify the multiplication.
$\frac{x + 6y^6}{2xy^7}$	Add the two numerators over the common denominator.

99. A: The point $(-3, -16)$ lies on the line that has a slope of 3 and that passes through $(1, -4)$. If $(-3, -16)$ is one of the endpoints of the line, the other would be $(5, 8)$.

100. B: Notice that $x = 1$ results in a zero in the denominator, so choice C cannot be correct since $x \neq 1$. To solve, subtract $\frac{2}{x-1}$ from both sides, then cross-multiply.

$\frac{x-2}{x-1} = \frac{x-1}{x+1} + \frac{2}{x-1}$	Write out the original equation.
$\frac{x-4}{x-1} = \frac{x-1}{x+1}$	Subtract $\frac{2}{x-1}$ from both sides.
$(x+1)(x-4) = (x-1)(x-1)$	Cross multiply.
$x^2 - 3x - 4 = x^2 - 2x + 1$	Multiply the binomials on both sides.
$-3x - 4 = -2x + 1$	Subtract x^2 from both sides.
$-4 = x + 1$	Add $3x$ to both sides.
$-5 = x$	Subtract 1 from both sides.

Practice Test #2

1. A manufacturer wishes to produce a cylindrical can which can hold up to 0.5 L of liquid. To the nearest tenth, what is the radius of the can which requires the least amount of material to make?

a. 2.8 cm
b. 4.3 cm
c. 5.0 cm
d. 9.2 cm

2. In ΔABC, $\cos A =$

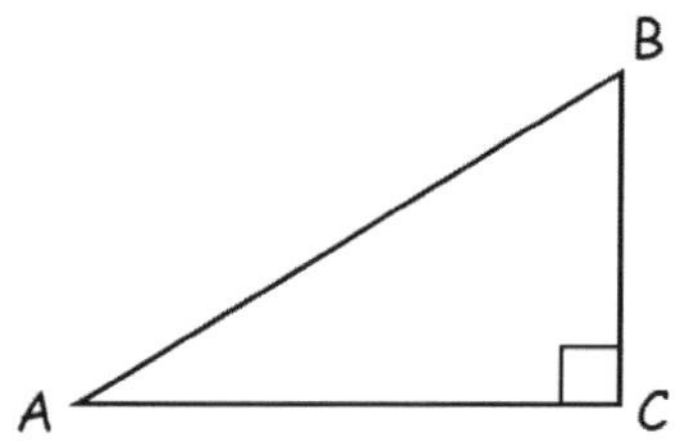

a. $\sin(90 - A)$
b. $\cos(90 - A)$
c. $\tan(90 - A)$
d. $\sec(90 - A)$

3. Which mathematician is responsible for the formula for vertices, edges, and faces of a geometric solid: $V - E + F = 2$?

a. Pythagoras
b. Euclid
c. Euler
d. Fermat

Refer to the following for questions 4–5:

Twenty-five children in a class are given an unevenly weighted six-sided die to see who can roll a six. Each child rolls the die twice and the teacher records how many sixes each child rolls.

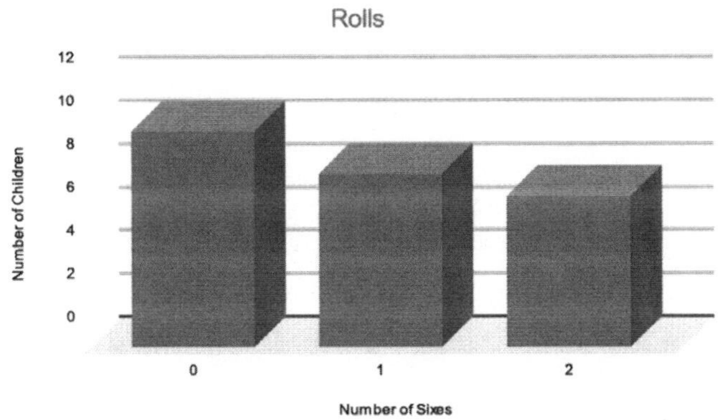

4. Given these experimental data, which of these approximates $P(\text{six})$ for a single roll of this die?

a. 0.22
b. 0.3
c. 0.44
d. 0.56

5. Which of these shows the graphs of the probability distributions (probability of rolling a six) from six rolls of this unevenly-weighted die and six rolls of a fair die?

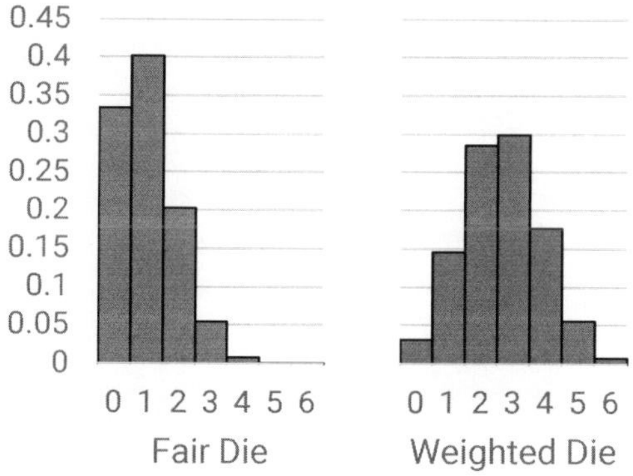

a.

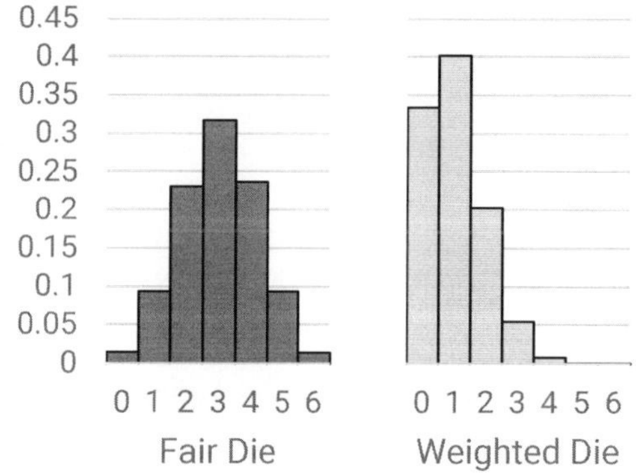

b.

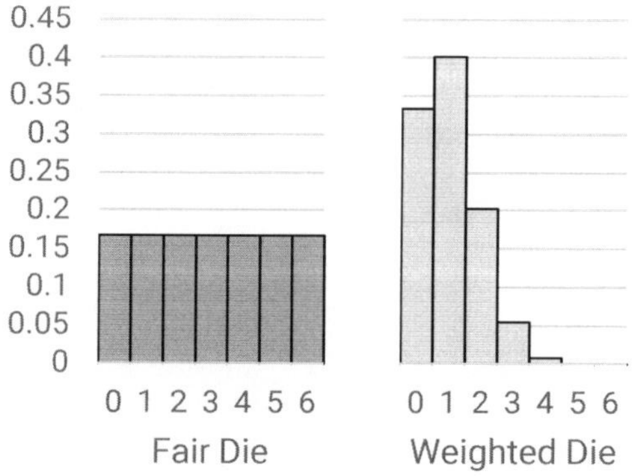

b.

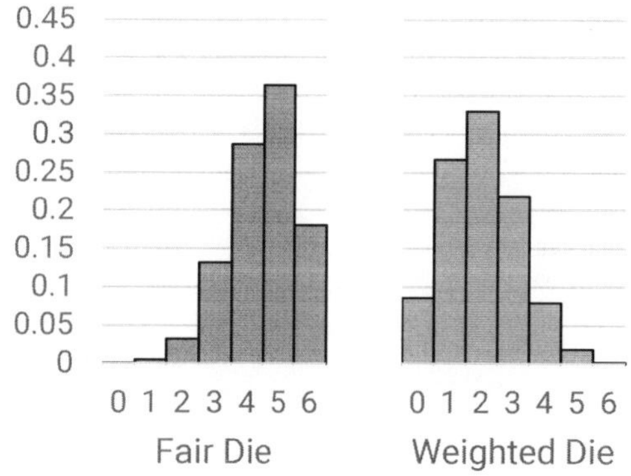

d.

6. For ΔABC, what is the length of $\overline{BC}$?

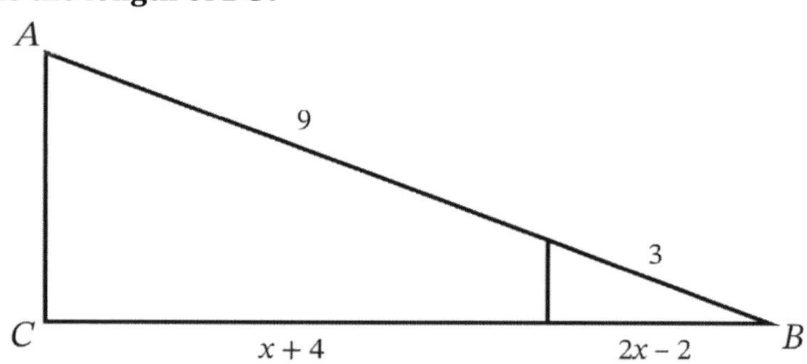

a. 2
b. 6
c. 8
d. 9

7. Milly walks x meters north and $x + 15$ meters east to get to the grocery store. On a neighborhood map which has a scale of 1 cm : 15 m, the distance between Milly's house and the grocery store is 5 cm. How far did Milly walk to the store?

a. 105 m
b. 75 m
c. 60 m
d. 45 m

8. Which of these graphs is representative of the data set shown below?

3 | 2 5 5
4 | 1 3 6 6 7
5 | 2 7 8
6 | 0 5 6 6 8

KEY
$2|123 = 21, 22, 23$

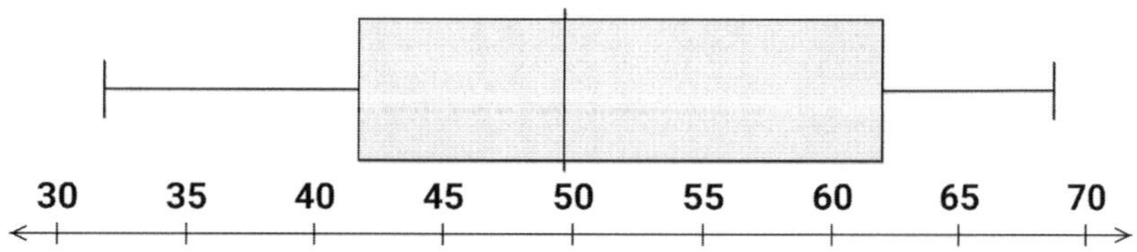

a.

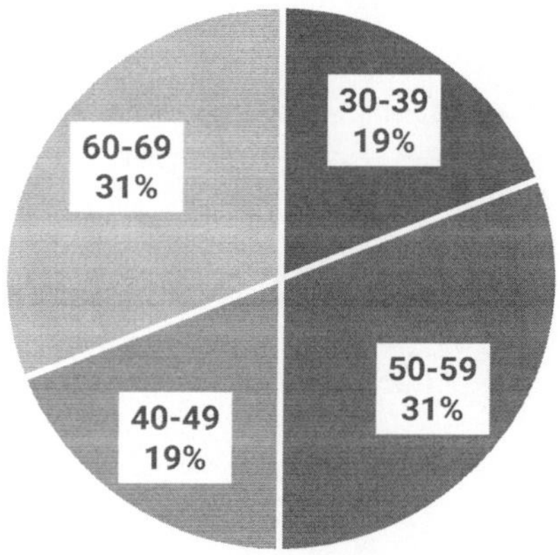

b.

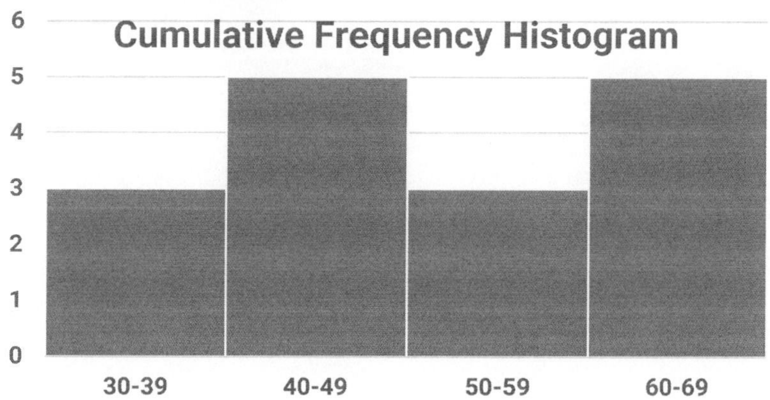

c.

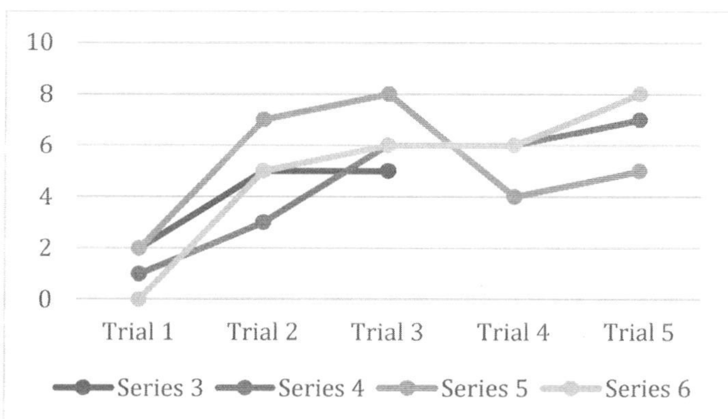

d.

9. To test the accuracy and precision of two scales, a student repeatedly measured the mass of a 5g standard and recorded these results.

	Trial 1	Trial 2	Trial 3	Trial 4
Scale 1	4.98 g	4.97 g	4.99 g	5.03 g
Scale 2	5.01 g	4.99 g	5.02 g	5.01 g

Which of these conclusions about the scales is true?

a. Scale 1 has an average percent error of 0.45%, and Scale 2 has an average percent error of 0.25%. Scale 2 is more accurate and precise than Scale 1.
b. Scale 1 has an average percent error of 0.45%, and Scale 2 has an average percent error of 0.25%. Scale 2 is more accurate than Scale 1; however, Scale 1 is more precise.
c. Scale 1 has an average percent error of 0.2%, and Scale 2 has an average percent error of 0.4%. Scale 1 is more accurate and precise than Scale 2.
d. Scale 1 has an average percent error of 0.2%, and Scale 2 has an average percent error of 0.4%. Scale 1 is more accurate than Scale 2; however, Scale 2 is more precise.

10. Simplify:

$$\begin{bmatrix} 1 & -3 & 2 \end{bmatrix}\left(\begin{bmatrix} -3 \\ 2 \\ 1 \end{bmatrix} + \begin{bmatrix} 3 \\ 4 \\ -2 \end{bmatrix}\right)$$

a. $\begin{bmatrix} 0 & -18 & -2 \end{bmatrix}$
b. $\begin{bmatrix} 0 \\ -18 \\ -2 \end{bmatrix}$
c. $\begin{bmatrix} -20 \end{bmatrix}$
d. $\begin{bmatrix} 1 & 0 & 0 \\ -3 & 0 & 6 \\ 2 & 0 & -1 \end{bmatrix}$

11. If a square root of twice the sum of x and 6 is equal to half of x, which of these is a possible value of x?

a. 12
b. $\frac{3}{2}$
c. $-3i$
d. -3

12. Which of these relationships represents y as a function of x?

a. $x^2 + y^2 = 16$

b.

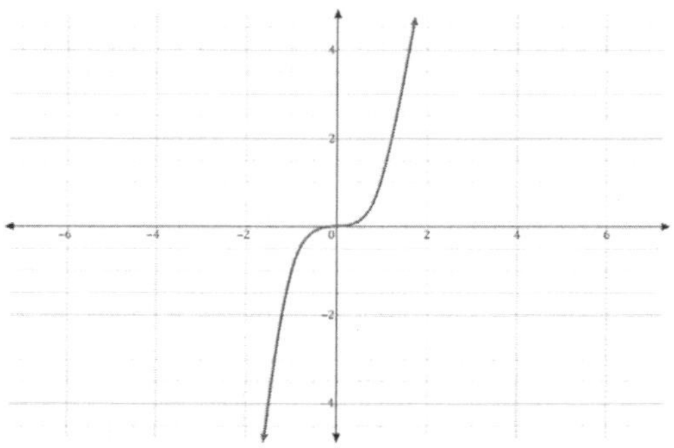

c. $y = \pm\sqrt{x}$

d.

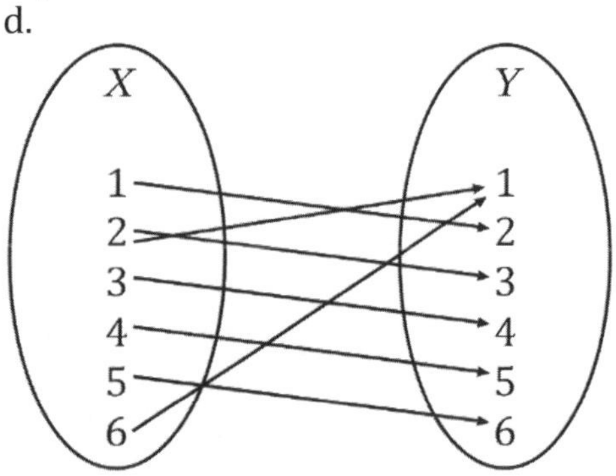

13. Two teachers from a county are chosen at random to attend a conference for high school science educators. What is the approximate probability that two women from the same department will be chosen?

	Biology	Chemistry	Physics
Women	26	31	20
Men	16	11	25

a. 8.6%
b. 10.7%
c. 11.9%
d. 13.8%

14. What is the contrapositive of the statement below?

If Bryan eats peanuts, he has an allergic reaction.

a. If Bryan eats peanuts, he does not have an allergic reaction.
b. If Bryan does not have an allergic reaction, he does not eat peanuts.
c. If Bryan does not eat peanuts, he does not have an allergic reaction.
d. If Bryan does not eat peanuts, he has an allergic reaction.

15. The test scores of 250 students are normally distributed with a mean score of 84 and a standard deviation of 7. In a normal distribution, approximately 68% of values are within one standard deviation of the mean. About how many students scored 91 or higher?

a. 16
b. 40
c. 88
d. 102

16. Which of these statements is NOT necessarily true when $f(x) = \log_b x$ and $b > 1$?

a. The x-intercept of the graph of $f(x)$ is $(1, 0)$.
b. The graph of $f(x)$ passes through $(b, 1)$.
c. $f(x) < 0$ when $0 < x < 1$.
d. If $g(x) = x^b$, the graph of $f(x)$ is symmetric to the graph of $g(x)$ with respect to $y = x$.

17. Which of the following is NOT an axiom of Euclidean geometry?

I. Between any two points, a single, straight line segment may be drawn.
II. On any given plane, a circle may be drawn.
III. Any given right angle is congruent to any other right angle.

a. I
b. II
c. I & III
d. I, II, & III

18. Solve the system of equations: $\begin{cases} -4x + 3y = 8 \\ 6x - 2y = -7 \end{cases}$.

a. $\left(\frac{1}{2}, \frac{10}{3}\right)$
b. $\left(-1, \frac{3}{2}\right)$
c. $(2, -\frac{5}{2})$
d. $\left(-\frac{1}{2}, 2\right)$

19. McKenzie shades $\frac{1}{5}$ of a piece of paper. Then, she shades an additional area $\frac{1}{5}$ the size of what she just shaded. Next, she shades another area $\frac{1}{5}$ as large as the previous one. As she continues the process to infinity, what is the limit of the shaded fraction of the paper?

a. $\frac{1}{5}$
b. $\frac{1}{4}$
c. $\frac{1}{3}$
d. $\frac{1}{2}$

20. Line segment $\overline{PQ}$ has endpoints (a, b) and (c, b). If $\overline{P'Q'}$ is the translation of $\overline{PQ}$ along a diagonal line such that P' is located at point (c, d), what is the area of quadrilateral $PP'Q'Q$?

a. $|a - c| \times |b - d|$
b. $|a - b| \times |c - d|$
c. $|a - d| \times |b - c|$
d. $(a - c)^2$

21. A small company is divided into three departments, as shown. Two individuals are chosen at random to attend a conference. What is the approximate probability that two women from the same department will be chosen?

	Department 1	Department 2	Department 3
Women	12	28	16
Men	18	14	15

a. 8.6%
b. 10.7%
c. 11.2%
d. 13.8%

22. As shown below, six congruent isosceles trapezoids are fitted together. Find the value of the angle x.

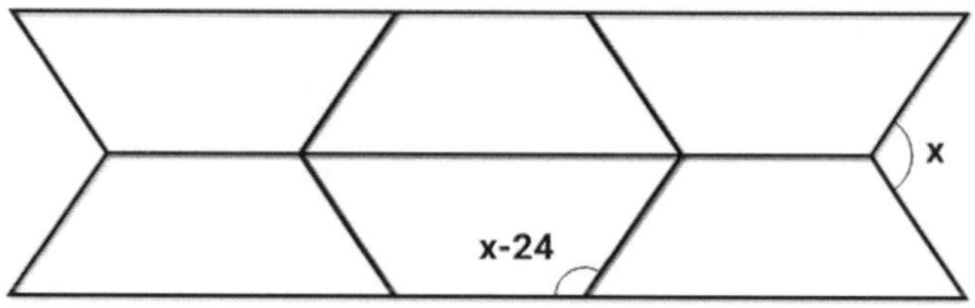

a. $x = 92°$
b. $x = 104°$
c. $x = 136°$
d. $x = 125°$

23. The ratio of revenue of new car sales to used car sales at the car lot is 3 : 5. If the total revenue of car sales was \$287,400 last month, what was the total revenue of the used car sales?

a. \$107,775
b. \$179,625
c. \$192,450
d. \$204,500

24. Solve the equation $2 - \sqrt{x} = \sqrt{x - 20}$.

a. $x = 6$
b. $x = 36$
c. $x = 144$
d. No solution

25. On a floor plan drawn at a scale of 1 : 100, the area of a rectangular room is 30 cm^2. What is the actual area of the room?

a. 30,000 cm^2
b. 300 m^2
c. 3,000 m^2
d. 30 m^2

26. Which of the following data can utilize both the median and mode?

I. Nominal Data
II. Interval Data
III. Ordinal Data

a. II only
b. III only
c. II and III
d. I, II, and III

27. In how many distinguishable ways can a family of five be seated at a circular table with five chairs if Tasha and Mac must be kept separated by at least one chair?

a. 6
b. 12
c. 24
d. 60

28. To which of the following sets of numbers does –4 NOT belong?

a. The set of whole numbers
b. The set of rational numbers
c. The set of integers
d. The set of real numbers

29. In the 1600s, Galileo Galilei studied the motion of pendulums and discovered that the period of a pendulum, the time it takes to complete one full swing, is a function of the square root of the length of its string: $2\pi\sqrt{\frac{L}{g}}$, where L is the length of the string and g is the acceleration due to gravity.

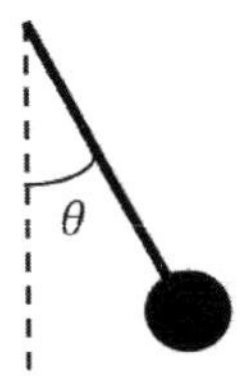

Consider two pendulums released from the same pivot point and at the same angle, $\theta = 30°$. Pendulum 1 has a mass of 100 g, while Pendulum 2 has a mass of 200 g. If Pendulum 1 has a period four times the period of Pendulum 2, what is true of the lengths of the pendulums' strings?

a. The length of Pendulum 1's string is four times the length of Pendulum 2's string.
b. The length of Pendulum 1's string is eight times the length of Pendulum 2's string.
c. The length of Pendulum 1's string is sixteen times the length of Pendulum 2's string.
d. The length of Pendulum 1's string is less than the length of Pendulum 2's string.

30. Ride Service A charges a flat rate of $10 for the first 10 miles, plus 25 cents per mile for anything over 10 miles. Ride Service B charges 40 cents per mile. Both services charge the same for a trip that is how long?

a. 40 miles
b. 45 miles
c. 50 miles
d. 55 miles

31. Jordan and Liz both live within walking distance of a skateboard park, as seen in the graphic below. How far apart are their homes, rounded to the nearest foot?

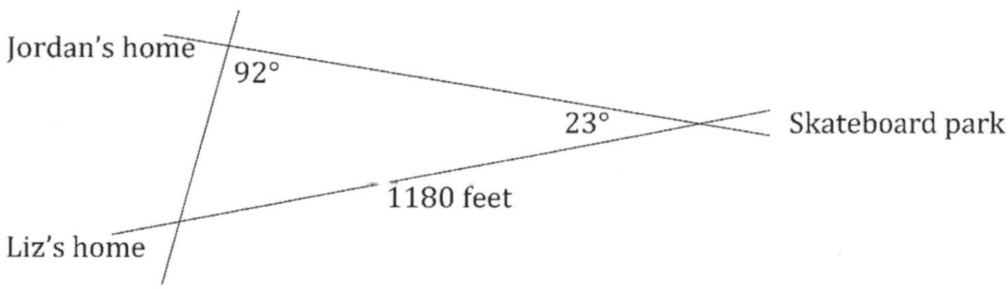

32. A greenhouse is built in the shape of a square pyramid. Each of the sides of the square base measures x ft, and the height is y feet. If the height were increased by 4 ft, how much more interior space would the greenhouse have?

a. $\frac{x^2y+4x^2}{3}$ ft^3
b. $\frac{y(x^2+4)}{3}$ ft^3
c. $\frac{4x^2}{3}$ ft^3
d. 64 ft^3

Refer to the following for question 33:

Below are graphed functions $f(x) = a_1 \sin(b_1 x)$ and $g(x) = a_2 \cos(b_2 x)$, where a_1 and a_2 are integers, and b_1 and b_2 are positive rational numbers.

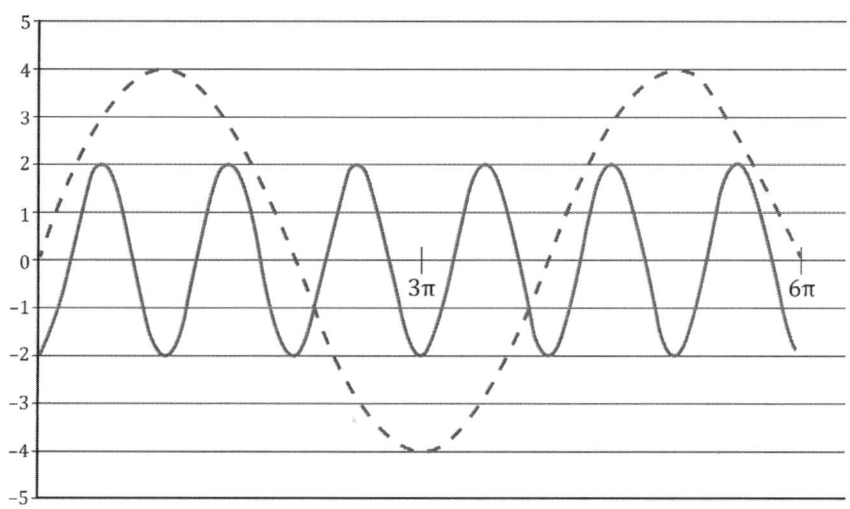

33. Which of the following statements is true?

a. $0 < a_2 < a_1$
b. $a_2 < 0 < a_1$
c. $0 < a_1 < a_2$
d. $a_2 < a_1 < 0$

34. Simplify:

$$\frac{(x^2y^{-3})(4xy)^2}{16x^4y^4}+\frac{3}{2xy}$$

a. $\frac{3x+24y^6}{8xy^7}$

b. $\frac{2x+6y^6}{2xy^4}$

c. $\frac{x+24y^5}{8xy^6}$

d. $\frac{2x+3y^4}{2xy^5}$

35. Which of the graphs below represents $f(x) = -3|-x+2|+$?

a. 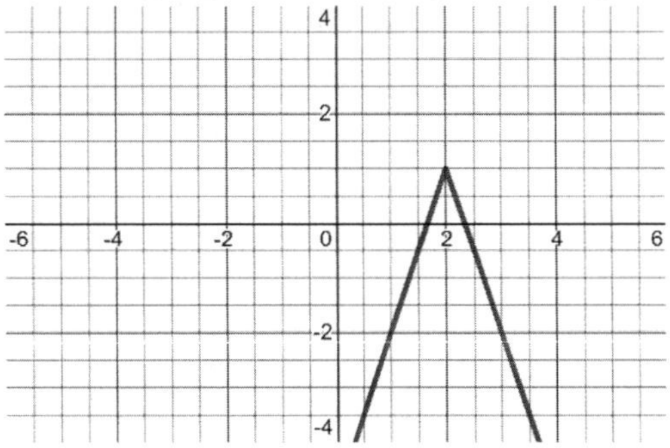

c. 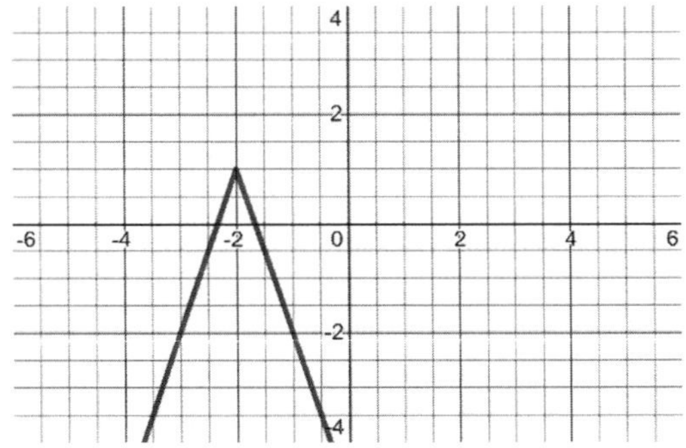

b. 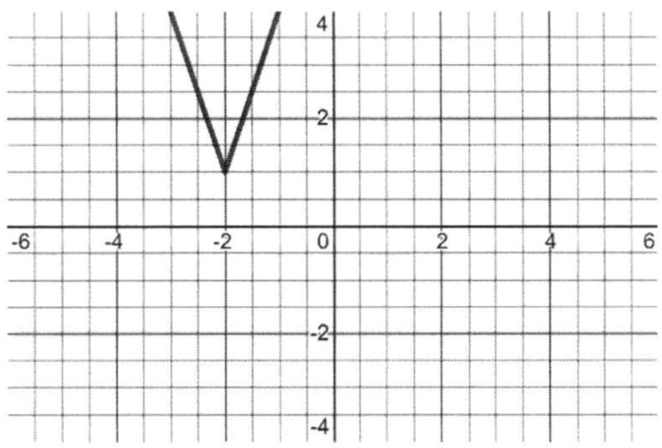

d. 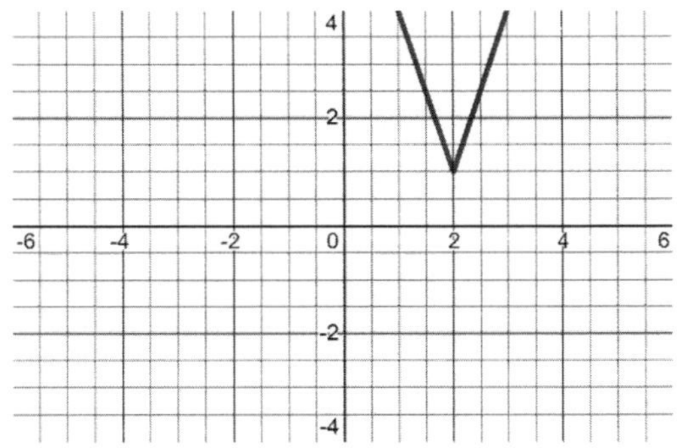

36. Which of these can be modeled by an exponential function?

a. The path of a sound wave
b. The path of a ball being kicked into the air
c. The distance an object travels over time when the rate is constant
d. Radioactive decay

37. Given this partial table of values for $f(x)$ and $g(x)$, find $f(g(-3))$. (Assume that $f(x)$ and $g(x)$ are the simplest polynomials that fit the data.)

x	$f(x)$	$g(x)$
-2	12	-6
-1	3	-4
0	0	-2
1	3	0
2	12	2
3		

a. 192
b. 104
c. 64
d. -8

38. Which of these is NOT a net of a cube?

a. b. c. d.

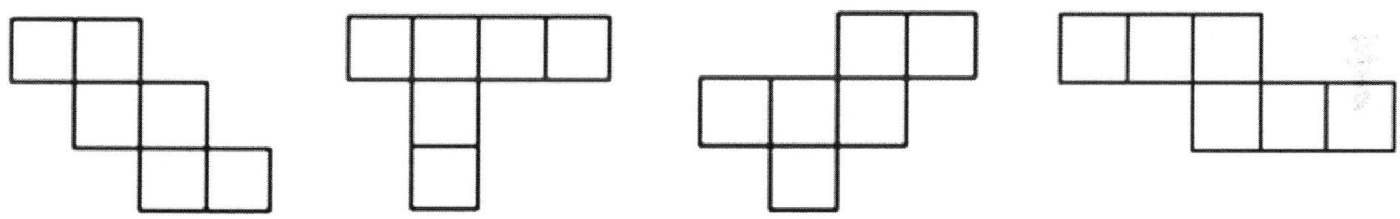

39. Which of these is a major contribution of the Greek civilization to the historical development of mathematics?

a. The division of an hour into 60 minutes, and a minute into 60 seconds, and a circle into 360 degrees
b. The development of algebra as a discipline separate from geometry
c. The use of deductive reasoning in geometric proofs
d. The introduction of Boolean logic

40. Given the function $f(x) = 10^x$. If $f(x) = 1$, which of these approximates x?

a. 0.1
b. 0
c. 1
d. 10

41. Mr. Aguilera needs 71 feet of fencing that costs \$3.98 per foot. Which of the following is the best approximation for the price of the fencing?

a. \$210
b. \$240
c. \$280
d. \$320

42. What is the period of the function $y = \tan(2x + 6)$?

a. $\frac{\pi}{2}$
b. π
c. 2π
d. 6π

43. Which number should come next in the sequence 7, 14, 28, 56, __?

a. 122
b. 112
c. 102
d. 84

44. Which numeral comes next in the sequence: 54, 59, 63, 68, 72, ...?

a. 76
b. 77
c. 78
d. 79

45. If $2\log_4 y + \log_4 16 = 3$, what is $\log_y 256$?

a. 16
b. 8
c. 4
d. 2

46. What is the radius of the circle defined by the equation $x^2 + y^2 - 4x + 6y - 5 = 0$?

a. $2\sqrt{3}$
b. $3\sqrt{2}$
c. $\sqrt{5}$
d. $2\sqrt{5}$

47. Ms. Robinson has a busy afternoon delivering gifts to family members. First, she drives 5.1 miles to her mother's house. Then, she drives 7.2 miles to her aunt's house, followed by 13.9 miles to her brother's house. Finally, she drives 14.6 miles on the return trip home. What is the best estimate of the total miles Ms. Robinson drives on her trip?

a. 29 miles
b. 41 miles
c. 39 miles
d. 42 miles

48. A random sample of 90 students at an elementary school were asked these three questions:

Do you like carrots?
Do you like broccoli?
Do you like cauliflower?

The results of the survey are shown below. If these data are representative of the population of students at the school, which of these is most probable?

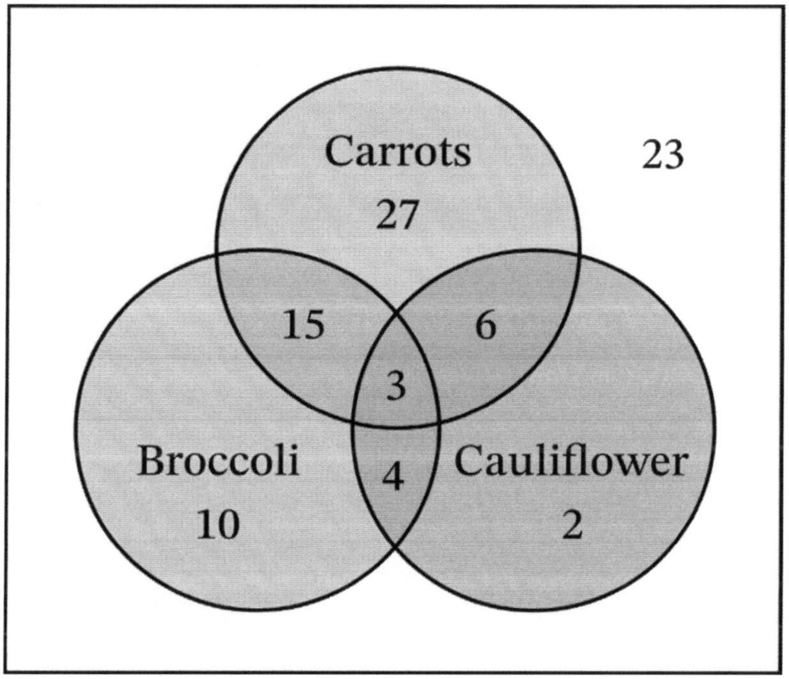

a. A student chosen at random likes broccoli.
b. Given a student chosen at random likes carrots, they will also like at least one other vegetable.
c. Given a student chosen at random likes cauliflower and broccoli, they will also like carrots.
d. A student chosen at random does not like carrots, broccoli, or cauliflower.

49. A circle is inscribed inside quadrilateral $ABCD$. $\overline{CB}$ is bisected by the point at which it is tangent to the circle. If $\overline{AB} = 6$, $\overline{BC} = 8$, and $\overline{DC} = 5$, then what is the length of $\overline{AD}$?

a. $\overline{AD} = 3$
b. $\overline{AD} = 2\sqrt{15}$
c. $\overline{AD} = 7$
d. $\overline{AD} = 9.5$

50. A teacher recorded the dates that students turned in projects in two different classes to compare trends and noticed that a large number of students were submitting their work late. She plotted charts to see how many students in each class were turning in late work and how late they were.

Which of the following is a true statement for these data?

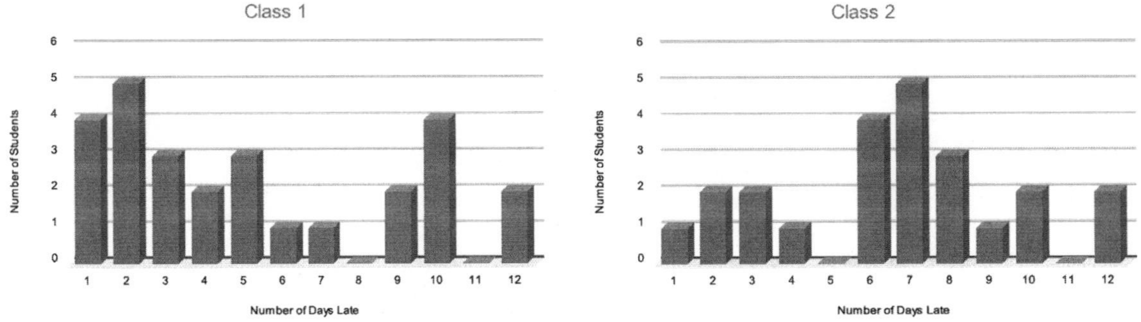

a. The median number of days late in Class 1 is 2 days less than in Class 2.
b. On average, students turned in work 4 days later in Class 2 than in Class 1 (round to nearest whole number).
c. The mode late time is higher for Class 2 than for Class 1.
d. The median late time for Class 1 is greater than the mean for Class 1.

51. Levi walked to the grocery store and back. The graph below shows his distance from home at times throughout the walk. If the y-axis represents the distance from home in miles and the x-axis represents the number of hours he was gone, which of the following statements is (are) true?

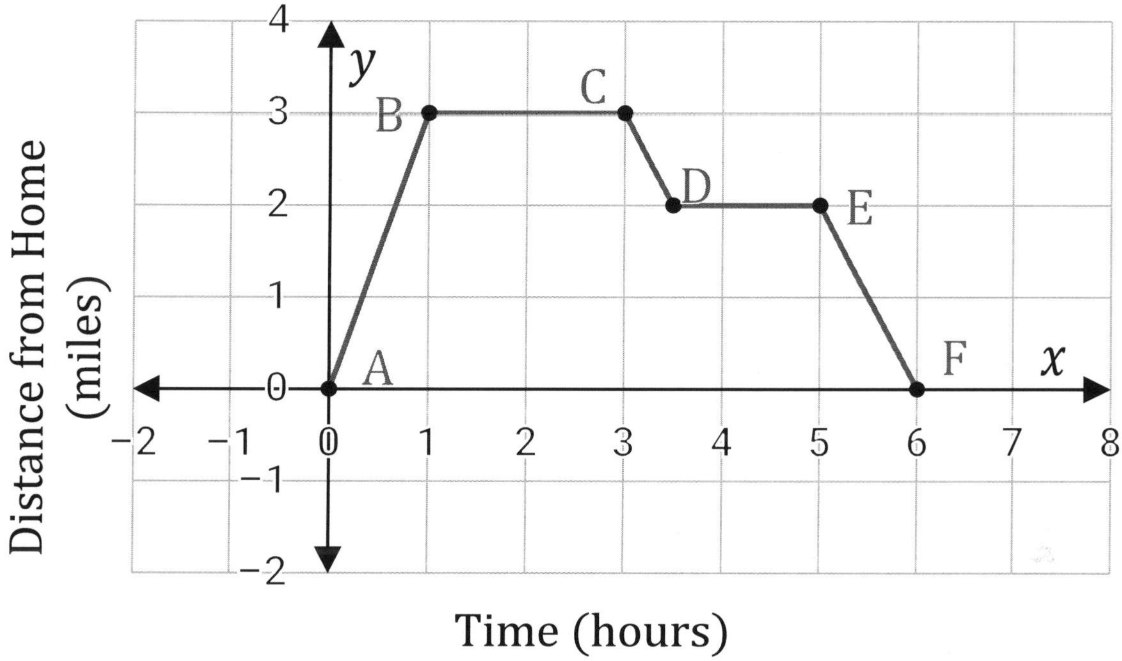

I. Levi's average speed was 1 mph.
II. Levi's speed from point A to point B was the same as from point E to F.
III. Levi walked a total distance of six miles.

a. I only
b. II only
c. I and II
d. I and III

52. Which of the following expressions gives the area *A* of the triangle below as a function of sides *a* and *b*?

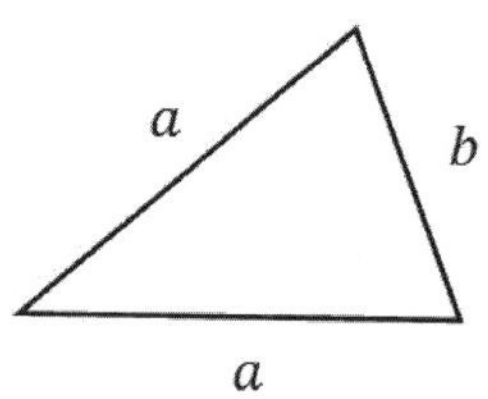

a. $\frac{2a^2-b^2}{4}$
b. $\frac{ab-a^2}{2}$
c. $\frac{b\sqrt{a^2-b^2}}{2}$
d. $\frac{b\sqrt{4a^2-b^2}}{4}$

53. Which of these can be modeled by a quadratic function?

a. The path of a sound wave
b. The path of a bullet
c. The distance an object travels over time when the rate is constant
d. Radioactive decay

54. What is the converse of the statement below?

If I go skiing, then it is winter.

a. If it is not winter, then I do not go skiing.
b. If it is winter, then I go skiing.
c. If it is not winter, then I go skiing.
d. If I go skiing, then it is not winter.

55. Find $f''(x)$ if $f(x) = -3x^3 - x^2 + 2x - 4$.

a. $-9x^2 - 2x + 2$
b. $-18x - 2$
c. $-27x^2 - 2x$
d. $-9x^3 - 2x^2 - 2x$

56. Jen sells honey from her beehive through two local grocery stores, as well as offering it online. The two local stores (Store A and Store B) charge $10.50 and $11.00 per pint, respectively. Jen receives 80% of the revenue from the local stores. She charges $6.75 per pint plus a $2.50 shipping fee for online shoppers (Store C). During a holiday, Store A offers a sale price of 25% off. Store B offers a coupon for $1.50 off. Jen offers a deal for free shipping. Which of the following lists the stores in order from lowest revenue to highest revenue that Jen receives during the holiday sale after all discounts and fees are applied?

a. Store A, Store C, Store B
b. Store B, Store C, Store A
c. Store C, Store A, Store B
d. Store C, Store B, Store A

57. Simplify: $(4 - i)^2 - (2 - 4i)$.

a. $\sqrt{185}$
b. $13 - 4i$
c. $13 + 4i$
d. 17

58. In a town of 35,638 people, about a quarter of the population is under the age of 35. Of those, just over a third attend local K–12 schools. If the number of students in each grade is about the same, how many fourth graders likely reside in the town?

a. Fewer than 100
b. Between 200 and 300
c. Between 300 and 400
d. More than 400

59. Lisa is selling brownies and cupcakes at a bake sale. Brownies cost \$2 each and cupcakes cost \$3 each. Lisa must sell at least \$150 worth of baked goods to break even on baking costs and the cost of renting the booth. If the x-axis represents the number of brownies sold and the y-axis represents the number of cupcakes sold, which of the following graphs shows the amount of baked goods Lisa must sell to break even or make a profit?

a.

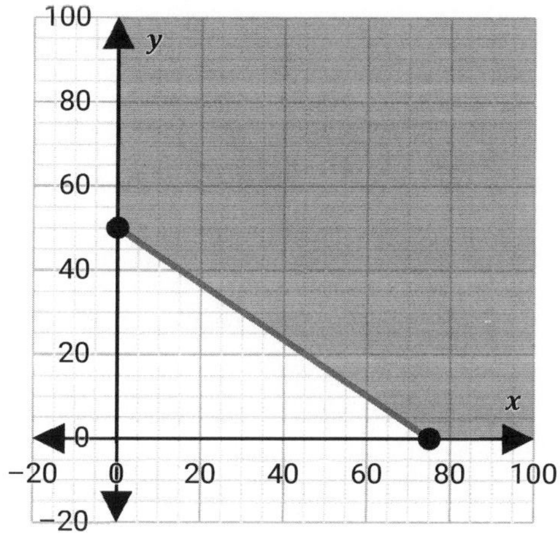

b.

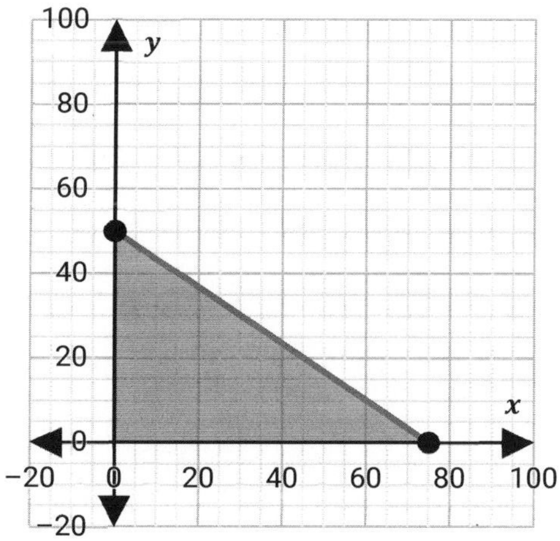

c.

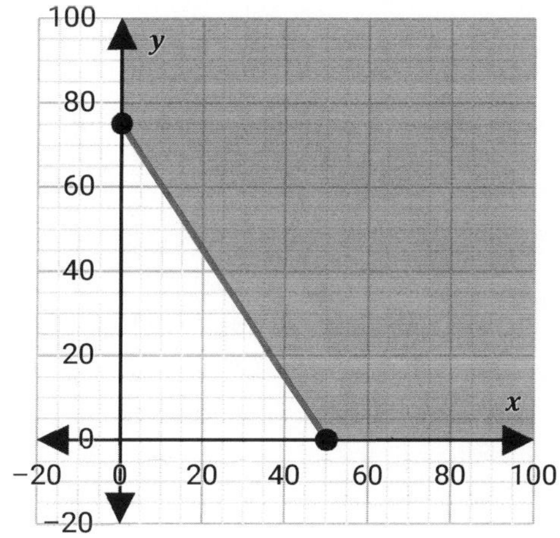

d.

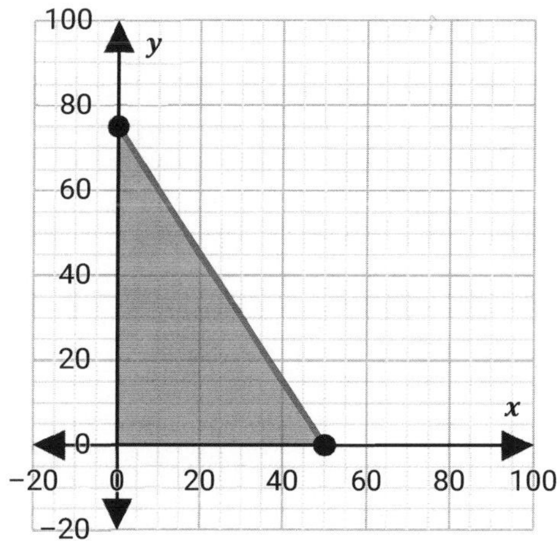

60. A cube inscribed in a sphere has a volume of 64 cubic units. What is the volume of the sphere in cubic units?

a. $4\pi\sqrt{3}$
b. $8\pi\sqrt{3}$
c. $32\pi\sqrt{3}$
d. $256\pi\sqrt{3}$

61. Gene P has three possible alleles, or gene forms, called a, b and c. Each individual carries two copies of Gene P, one of which is inherited from his or her mother and the other of which is inherited from his or her father. If the two copies of Gene P are of the same form, the individual is homozygous for that allele; otherwise, the individual is heterozygous. The following table represents genetic data from 500 individuals selected at random from the population.

		Allele 2		
		a	b	c
Allele 1	a	6	10	39
	b	11	21	79
	c	36	65	233

Using experimental probability, predict the number of individuals in a population of 100,000 who will be homozygous for either the a or b allele.

a. 2,800
b. 5,000
c. 5,400
d. 9,000

62. A random sample of 241 children ages 5 to 10 were asked these three questions:

Do you like baseball?
Do you like basketball?
Do you like football?

The results of the survey are shown below. If these data are representative of the population of students at the school, which of these is least probable?

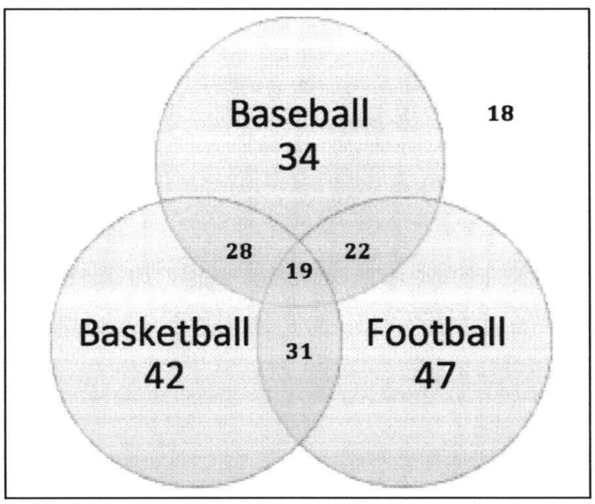

a. A child chosen at random likes football.
b. If a child chosen at random likes baseball, he also likes at least one other sport.
c. If a child chosen at random likes baseball and basketball, he also likes football.
d. A student chosen at random does not like baseball, basketball, or football.

63. Which of these equations most closely resembles the graph below?

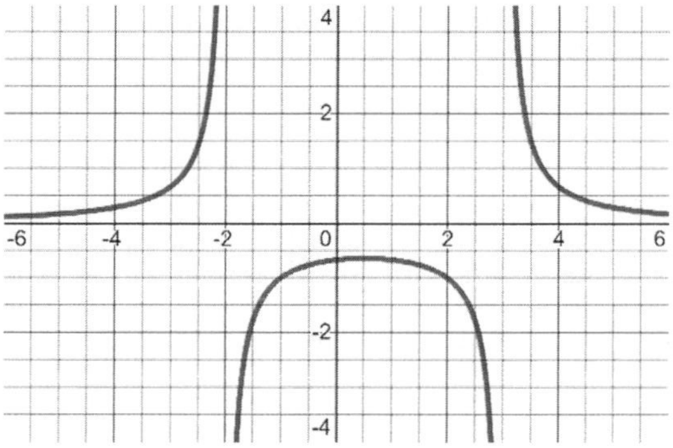

a. $y = \frac{2x+4}{x^2-x-6}$
b. $y = \frac{4}{x^2-x-6}$
c. $y = \frac{2}{x+2} + \frac{2}{x-3}$
d. $y = \frac{x+4}{x^2-x-3}$

64. Simplify: $\frac{4+i}{3-2i}$

a. $\frac{10}{13} + \frac{11}{13}i$
b. $\frac{21}{13}$
c. $\frac{14}{13} + \frac{11}{13}i$
d. $\frac{10}{13} + \frac{5}{13}i$

65. Which of these statements is NOT necessarily true when $f(x) = \log_b x$ and $b > 1$?

a. The x-intercept of the graph of $f(x)$ is 0.
b. The graph of $f(x)$ passes through $(b, 1)$
c. $f(x) < 0$ when $0 < x < 1$
d. If $g(x) = b^x$, the graph of $f(x)$ is symmetric to the graph of $g(x)$ with respect to $y = x$.

66. To which of the following sets of numbers does $\sqrt{32}$ NOT belong?

I. The set of real numbers
II. The set of rational numbers
III. The set of complex numbers

a. I
b. II only
c. I and III
d. I, II, & III

67. A circle is inscribed inside quadrilateral $ABCD$. $\overline{CD}$ is bisected by the point at which it is tangent to the circle. If $\overline{AB} = 14$, $\overline{BC} = 10$, $\overline{CD} = 8$, then which of the following statements is true?

a. $\overline{AD} = 11$
b. $\overline{AD} = 2\sqrt{34}$
c. $\overline{AD} = 12$
d. $\overline{AD} = 17.5$

68. Which of these functions includes –1 as an element of the domain and –2 as an element of the range?

a. $y = \frac{1}{x-1} - 2$
b. $y = \frac{\sqrt{x-1}}{4} + 4$
c. $y = |x - 1| - 1$
d. $y = \begin{cases} x - 5 & x < -1 \\ -x + 1 & x \geq -1 \end{cases}$

69. Solve $\sqrt{2x} - 3 = \sqrt{2x - 15}$.

a. $x = 0$
b. $x = 4$
c. $x = 8$
d. $x = 10$

70. How many different 5-character passwords can be created with three letters (letters may be repeated) followed by two unique even digits?

a. 351,520
b. 672,480
c. 1,404,000
d. 1,581,840

71. Which of these does NOT simulate randomly selecting a student from a group of 11 students?

a. Assigning each student a unique card value of A, 2, 3, 4, 5, 6, 7, 8, 9, 10, or J, removing queens and kings from a standard deck of 52 cards, shuffling the remaining cards, and drawing a single card from the deck
b. Assigning each student a unique number 0–10 and using a computer to randomly generate a number within that range
c. Assigning each student a unique number from 2 to 12, rolling two dice, and finding the sum of the numbers on the dice
d. All of these can be used as a simulation of the event.

72. If a, b, and c are multiples of 3 and $4a^2 + b^3 = c$, which of these is the largest number that must be factor of c?

a. 3
b. 6
c. 9
d. 12

73. A triangle with vertices $A(-4,2)$, $B(-1,3)$, and $C(-5,7)$ is reflected across $y = -x + 1$ to give $\Delta A'B'C'$, which is subsequently reflected across the y-axis to give $\Delta A''B''C''$. Which of these statements is true?

a. A 90° rotation of ΔABC about (0,1) gives $\Delta A''B''C''$.
b. A reflection of ΔABC about the x-axis gives $\Delta A''B''C''$.
c. A 270° rotation of ΔABC about (0,1) gives $\Delta A''B''C''$.
d. A translation of ΔABC one unit down gives $\Delta A''B''C''$.

74. The two prisms shown below are similar (units are inches). What is the measure of x?

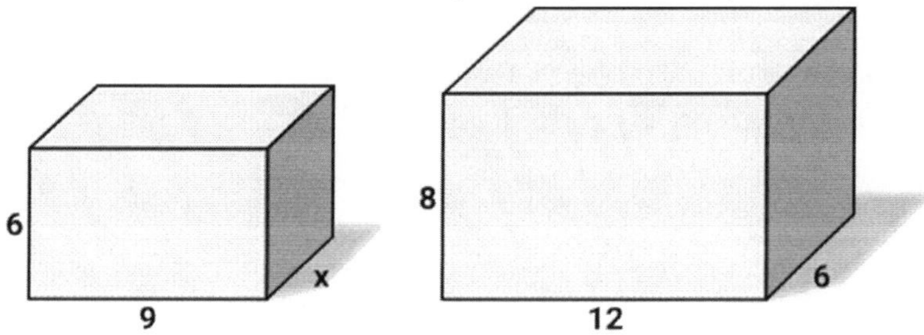

a. $4\frac{1}{2}$ in
b. $4\frac{3}{4}$ in
c. 5 in
d. $5\frac{1}{4}$ in

75. Which of these could be the equation of the function graphed below?

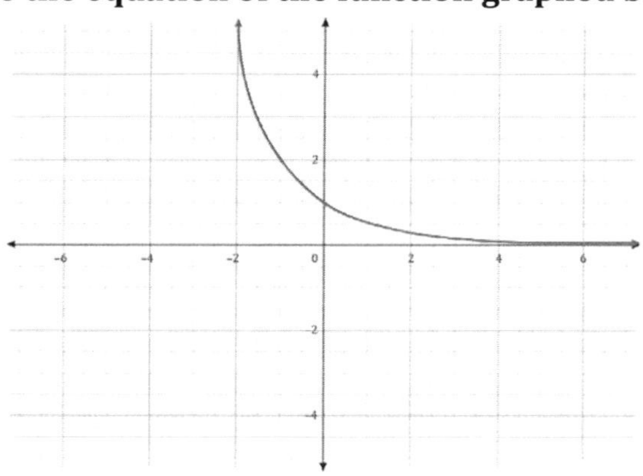

a. $f(x) = x^2$
b. $f(x) = \sqrt{x}$
c. $f(x) = 2^{-x}$
d. $f(x) = \log_2 x$

76. Identify a possible cross section formed by a plane containing the given points on the cylinder.

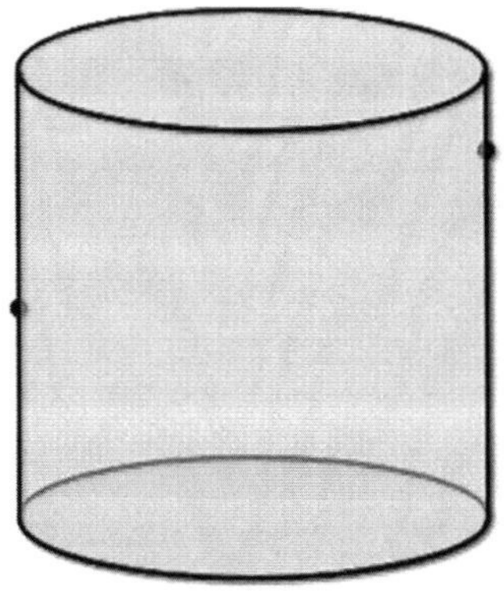

a. Circle
b. Ellipse
c. Parabola
d. Triangle

77. A homeowner is ordering fencing material to place a fence around her property. The lot is rectangular with a length of 385 feet, and the width is 295 feet. Which of the following is the best estimate of the minimum amount of fencing material she should order?

a. 1600 feet
b. 700 feet
c. 1,400 feet
d. 1,200 feet

78. A man looks out of a window of a tall building at a 45° angle of depression and sees his car in the parking lot. When he turns his gaze downward to a 60° angle of depression, he sees his wife's car. If his car is parked 60 feet from his wife's car, about how far from the building did his wife park her car?

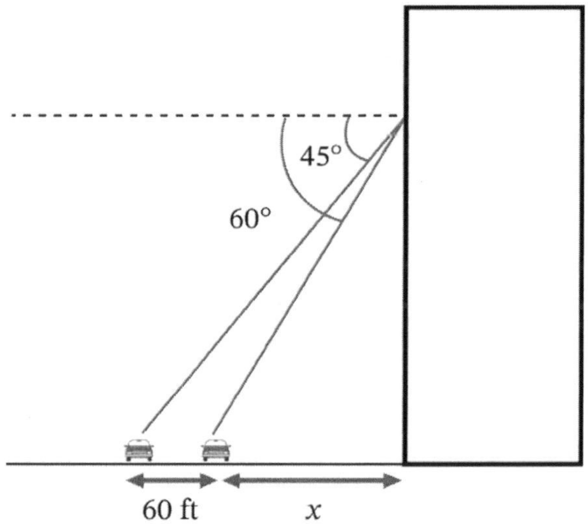

a. 163 feet
b. 122 feet
c. 82 feet
d. 60 feet

79. If $\sin\theta = \frac{1}{2}$ when $\frac{\pi}{2} < \theta < \pi$, what is the value of θ?

a. $\frac{\pi}{6}$
b. $\frac{\pi}{3}$
c. $\frac{2\pi}{3}$
d. $\frac{5\pi}{6}$

80. Which of the following piecewise functions can describe the graph below?

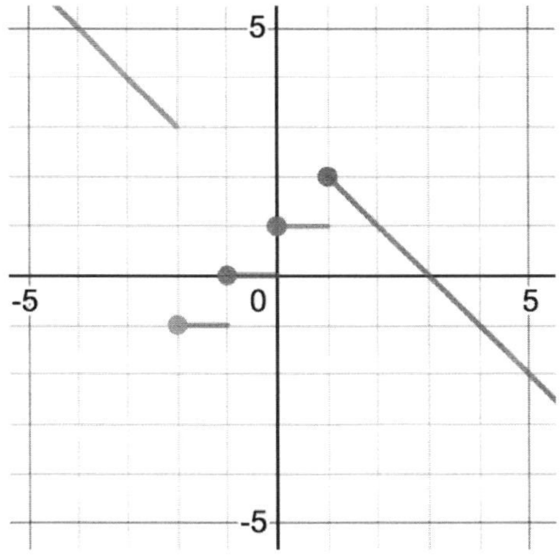

a. $f(x) = \begin{cases} -x+1 & x < -2 \\ [\![x]\!] & -2 \le x < 1 \\ -2x+3 & x \ge 1 \end{cases}$

b. $f(x) = \begin{cases} -x+1 & x \le -2 \\ [\![x+1]\!] & -2 \le x < 1 \\ -x+3 & x \ge 1 \end{cases}$

c. $f(x) = \begin{cases} -x+1 & x < -2 \\ [\![x]\!]+1 & -2 \le x < 1 \\ -x+3 & x \ge 2 \end{cases}$

d. $f(x) = \begin{cases} -x+1 & x \le -2 \\ [\![x-1]\!] & -2 < x \le 1 \\ -2x+6 & x > 1 \end{cases}$

81. Gene Y has three possible alleles, or gene forms, called a, b and c. Each individual carries two copies of Gene Y, one of which is inherited from his or her mother and the other of which is inherited from his or her father. If the two copies of Gene Y are of the same form, the individual is homozygous for that allele; otherwise, the individual is heterozygous. The following table represents genetic data from 1,000 individuals selected at random from the population.

		Allele 2		
		a	**b**	**c**
Allele 1	**a**	136	72	29
	b	132	213	141
	c	32	65	180

Using experimental probability, predict the number of individuals in a population of 10,000 who will be homozygous for any allele.

a. 4,710
b. 4,920
c. 5,080
d. 5,290

82. Which of these statements is true for functions $f(x)$, $g(x)$, and $h(x)$?

$$f(x) = 2x - 2$$
$$g(x) = 2x^2 - 2$$
$$h(x) = 2x^3 - 2$$

a. The degree of each polynomial function is 2.
b. The leading coefficient of each function is –2.
c. Each function has exactly one real zero at $x = 1$.
d. None of these is true for functions $f(x)$, $g(x)$, and $h(x)$.

83. Solve $4x^3y^2 - 16x^2y = -16x^3y + 4x^2y^2$ for x.

a. $x = \{0\}$
b. $x = \{0,1\}$
c. $x = \{-4\}$
d. $x = \{-4,0,1\}$

84. Solve $x^4 + 9 = 10x^2$.

a. $x = \{1, 3\}$
b. $x = \{-3i, -i, i, 3i\}$
c. $x = \{i, 3i\}$
d. $x = \{-3, -1, 1, 3\}$

Refer to the following for questions 85–87:

The box-and-whisker plot displays student test scores by class period.

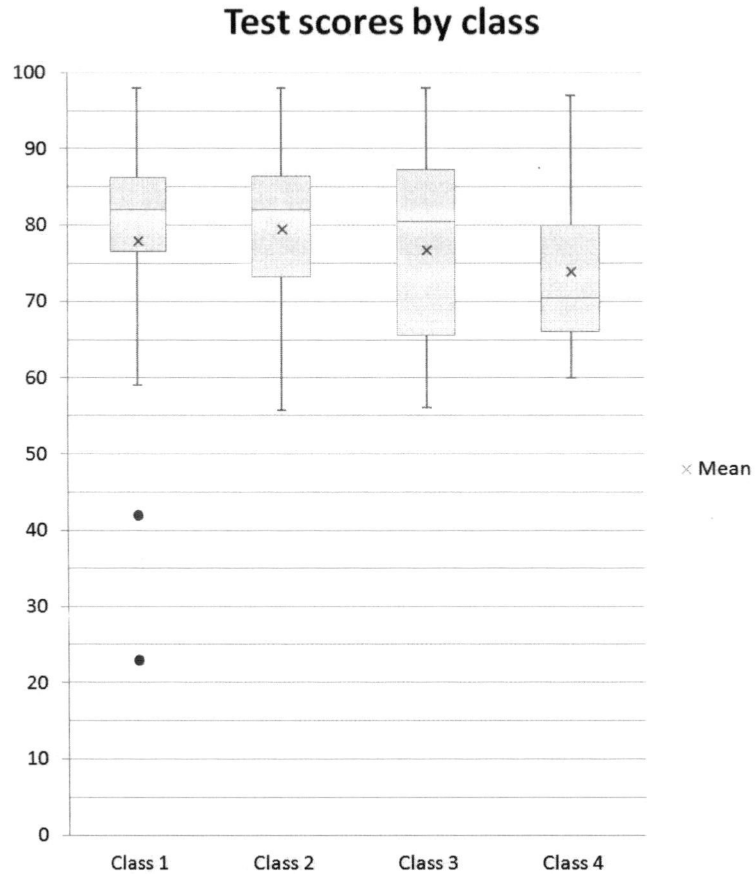

85. Which of the following statements is true of the data?

a. The mean better reflects student performance in class 1 than the median.
b. The mean test score for class 1 and 2 is the same.
c. The median test score for class 1 and 2 is the same.
d. The median test score is above the mean for class 4.

86. What is the probability that a student chosen at random from class 2 made above a 73 on this test?

a. 0.25
b. 0.5
c. 0.6
d. 0.75

87. Which class has the greatest range of test scores?

a. Class 1
b. Class 2
c. Class 3
d. Class 4

88. Simplify $\sqrt{\frac{-32x^4}{75y^5}}$.

a. $\frac{2x^2i\sqrt{2y}}{9y^3}$
b. $\frac{4x^2i\sqrt{6y}}{15y^3}$
c. $\frac{-2x^2\sqrt{21y}}{9y^3}$
d. $\frac{8x^3i\sqrt{6y}}{27y^2}$

89. A pair of jeans is marked down 30% and placed on a clearance rack, on which is posted a sign reading, "Take an extra 15% off already reduced merchandise." What fraction of the original price is the final sale price of the jeans?

a. $\frac{61}{100}$
b. $\frac{119}{200}$
c. $\frac{4}{7}$
d. $\frac{3}{5}$

90. The heights of 200 high school males are normally distributed with a mean height of 67.5 inches and a standard deviation of 3.5 inches. In a normal distribution, approximately 68% of values are within one standard deviation of the mean. About how many individuals from the selected group are shorter than 5'11"?

a. 125
b. 142
c. 168
d. 184

91. Which of these represents the equation of a sphere that is centered in the xyz-space at the point $(1, 0, -2)$ and has a volume of 36π cubic units?

a. $x^2 + y^2 + z^2 - 2x + 4z = 4$
b. $x^2 + y^2 + z^2 + 2x - 4z = 4$
c. $x^2 + y^2 + z^2 - 2x + 4z = -2$
d. $x^2 + y^2 + z^2 + 2x - 4z = 2$

92. Solve: $\frac{x+2}{x+1} = \frac{x+9}{x+7} + \frac{2}{x+1}$.

a. $x = -3$
b. $x = -1$
c. $x = 1$
d. $x = 5$

93. Which of these would best illustrate change over time?

a. Pie chart
b. Line graph
c. Box-and-whisker plot
d. Venn diagram

Refer to the following for question 94:

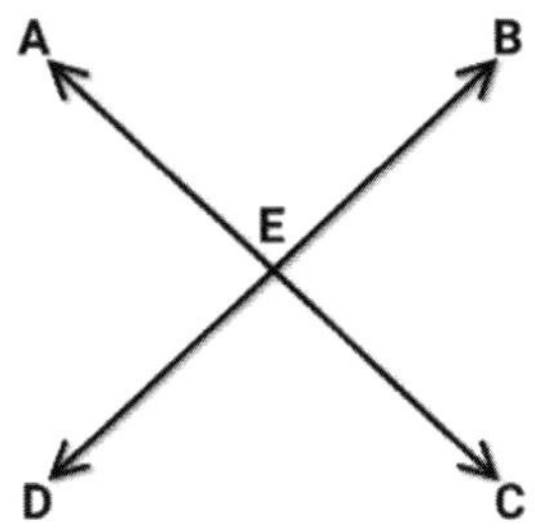

Statement	Reason
1. $\angle BEA \cong \angle DEA$	Given
2. $\angle BEA + \angle DEA = 180°$	Linear pair angles add up to 180°
3. ________	Substitution
4. $2 \times \angle BEA = 180°$	Combine like terms
5. $\angle BEA = 90°$	Division property of equality
6. $\angle BEA$ is a right angle	Definition of right angle
7. $\overleftrightarrow{BD} \perp \overleftrightarrow{AC}$	________

Given: $\angle BEA \cong \angle DEA$
Prove: $\overleftrightarrow{BD} \perp \overleftrightarrow{AC}$

■

94. Which of the following justifies step 7 in the proof?

a. ASA
b. Corresponding parts of congruent triangles are congruent
c. Definition of supplementary angles
d. Definition of perpendicular lines

95. Which of these is the least biased sampling technique?

a. A PE teacher records the height of the entire girls' volleyball team to show that the average height of high school girls today is greater than it was 50 years ago.
b. A woman surveys her entire neighborhood for opinions on the new business coming to town.
c. A news website requests feedback via an anonymous online form.
d. A journalist calls the first 50 names on a randomly generated list of all voters in the county to request opinions on a politician.

96. A student is asked to find 3/5 of 75. Which of the following expressions could the student use?

a. $(3 \times 75) \div 5$
b. $75 \div 0.6$
c. Either A or B
d. Neither A nor B

97. The game commission releases 16 wolves into a state park. The number of wolves over the next several years is shown on the table below:

Years after release	0	1	2	3
Number of wolves	16	24	36	54

How many wolves should the game commission expect to find 4 years after the release of the original 16 wolves?

a. 72
b. 81
c. 66
d. 62

98. Mr. Foster wants to put new carpet on the floor of his rectangular playroom. The playroom is 27 feet long and 18 feet wide. He has found an inexpensive carpet that is priced $14 per square yard. What would be a reasonable price for enough carpet to cover the floor of his playroom?

a. $486
b. $756
c. $1,260
d. $2,268

99. A chest is filled with large gold and silver coins, weighing a total of 30 pounds. If each gold coin weighs 12 ounces, each silver coin weighs 8 ounces, and there are 50 coins in all, how many gold coins does the chest contain? (There are 16 ounces in a pound.)

a. 10 coins
b. 15 coins
c. 20 coins
d. 30 coins

100. Which of the following represents the net of a triangular prism?

a. 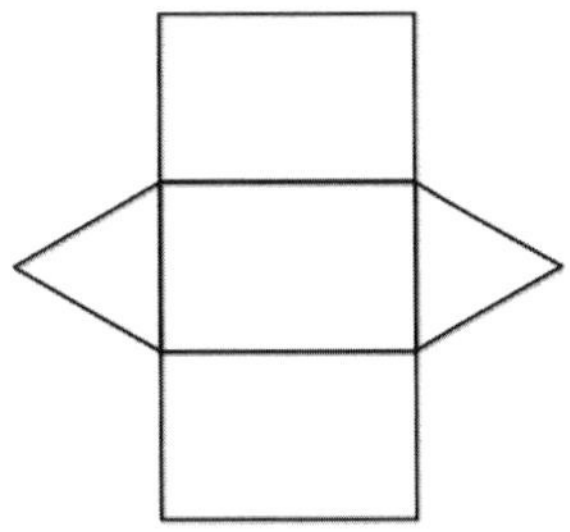

b. 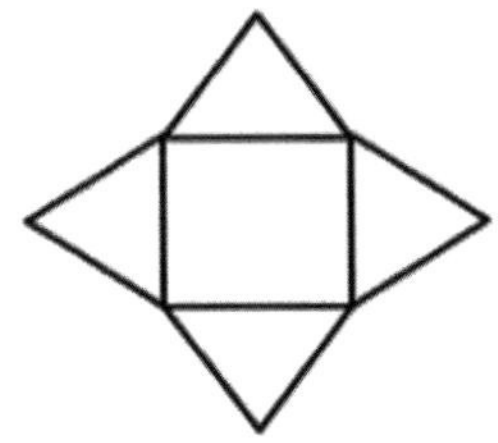

c. 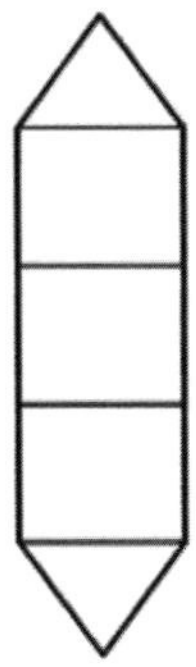

d. 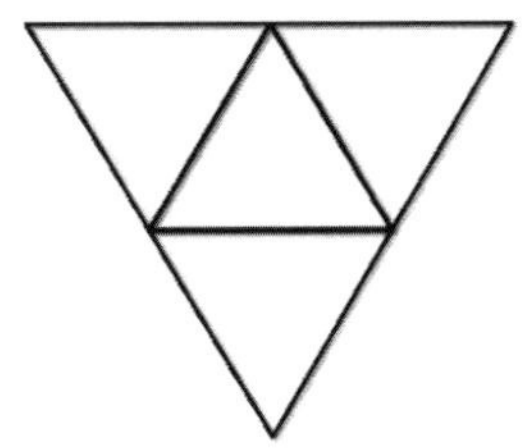

Answer Key and Explanations for Test #2

1. B: The manufacturer wishes to minimize the surface area A of the can while keeping its volume V fixed at $0.5 \text{ L} = 500 \text{ mL} = 500 \text{ cm}^3$. The formula for the surface area of a cylinder is $A = 2\pi rh + 2\pi r^2$, and the formula for volume is $V = \pi r^2 h$. To combine the two formulas into one, solve the volume formula for r or h and substitute the resulting expression into the surface area formula for r or h. The volume of the cylinder is 500 cm^3, so $500 = \pi r^2 h$ becomes $h = \frac{500}{\pi r^2}$. Therefore, $A = 2\pi rh + 2\pi r^2$ becomes $2\pi r\left(\frac{500}{\pi r^2}\right) + 2\pi r^2 = \frac{1{,}000}{r} + 2\pi r^2$. Find the critical point(s) by setting the first derivative equal to zero and solving for r. Note that r represents the radius of the can and must therefore be a positive number.

$$A = 1{,}000r^{-1} + 2\pi r^2$$
$$A' = -1{,}000r^{-2} + 4\pi r$$
$$0 = -\frac{1{,}000}{r^2} + 4\pi r$$
$$\frac{1{,}000}{r^2} = 4\pi r$$
$$1{,}000 = 4\pi r^3$$
$$\sqrt[3]{\frac{1{,}000}{4\pi}} = r$$
$$r \approx 4.3 \text{ cm}$$

So, when $r \approx 4.3$ cm, the minimum surface area is obtained. When the radius of the can is 4.3 cm, its height is $h \approx \frac{500}{\pi(4.3)^2} \approx 8.6$ cm, and surface area is approximately $\frac{1{,}000}{4.3} + 2\pi(4.3)^2 \approx 348.73 \text{ cm}^2$. Confirm that the surface area is greater when the radius is slightly smaller or larger than 4.3 cm. For instance, when $r = 4$ cm, the surface area is approximately 350.5 cm^2, and when $r = 4.5$ cm, the surface area is approximately 349.5 cm^2.

2. A: The cosine function is represented by the ratio $\frac{adjacent\ leg}{hypotenuse}$. In ΔABC, this can be written as $\frac{AC}{AB}$. The sine function is represented by the ratio $\frac{opposite\ leg}{hypotenuse}$. The sine of angle B can also be written as $\frac{AC}{AB}$. Since this is a right triangle, angles A and B are complementary (meaning they add up to 90°); therefore, angle B can be written as $90° - A$. It therefore follows that $\cos A = \sin(90 - A)$. Answer B gives the cosine of angle B, or $\frac{BC}{AB}$. Answer C gives the tangent of angle B, which is represented by the ratio $\frac{opposite\ leg}{adjacent\ leg}$, or $\frac{AC}{BC}$. Answer D gives the secant of angle B, which is the reciprocal of the cosine and is represented by the ratio $\frac{hypotenuse}{adjacent\ leg}$, or $\frac{AB}{BC}$.

3. C: Leonhard Euler made many important contributions to the field of mathematics. This includes the formula for calculating the number of vertices, edges, and faces on a geometric solid.

4. C: We count the number of sixes that were rolled and divide by the number of total rolls to find the probability.

$$\frac{8 \times 1 + 7 \times 2}{25 \times 2} = \frac{22}{50} = \frac{11}{25} = 0.44$$

5. A: To find the probability of rolling a six a certain number of times, use the formula:

$$({}_n\mathrm{C}_r)p^r q^{n-r}$$

For example, to find the probability of rolling a six four times in six rolls with a fair die:

$$({}_n\mathrm{C}_r)p^r q^{n-r} = ({}_6\mathrm{C}_4)(0.167)^4(0.833)^2 = \frac{6!}{2!\,4!}(0.167)^4(0.833)^2 \approx 0.008$$

To find the probability of rolling a six four times with the weighted die:

$$({}_n\mathrm{C}_r)p^r q^{n-r} = ({}_6\mathrm{C}_4)(0.44)^4(0.56)^2 = \frac{6!}{2!\,4!}(0.44)^4(0.56)^2 \approx 0.176$$

The calculated probabilities match those shown in choice A.

6. C: ΔABC is similar to the smaller triangle with which it shares vertex B.

$$\overline{BC} = (2x - 2) + (x + 4) = 3x + 2$$
$$\overline{AB} = 3 + 9 = 12$$

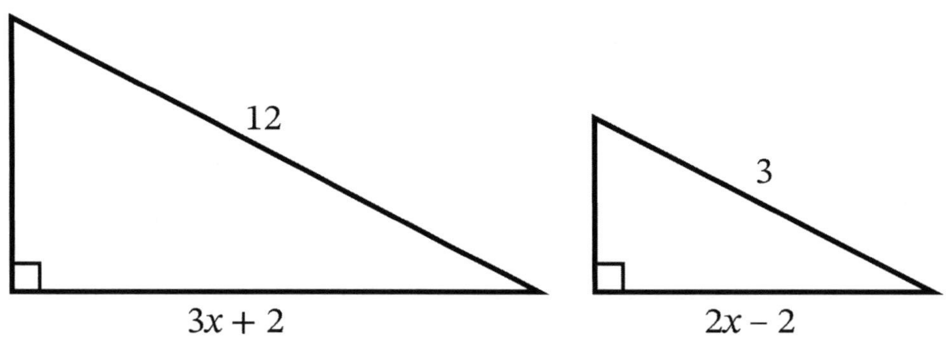

Set up a proportion and solve for x:

$$\frac{3x + 2}{12} = \frac{2x - 2}{3}$$
$$9x + 6 = 24x - 24$$
$$30 = 15x$$
$$x = 2$$

So, $BC = 3x + 2 = 3(2) + 2 = 8$.

7. A: If the distance is 5 cm on the map, then the actual distance is $5 \times 15 = 75$ m. To find x, use the Pythagorean theorem.

$$\begin{aligned} x^2 + (x + 15)^2 &= (75)^2 \\ x^2 + x^2 + 30x + 225 &= 5{,}625 \\ 2x^2 + 30x - 5{,}400 &= 0 \\ 2(x^2 + 15x - 2{,}700) &= 0 \\ 2(x - 45)(x + 60) &= 0 \\ x = 45 \quad x &= -60 \end{aligned}$$

Since x represents a distance in this situation, use the positive value. Since $x = 45$, $x + 15 = 60$. Milly walks a total of $45 + 60 = 105$ m to get to the store.

8. A: To draw a box-and-whisker plot from the data, find the median, quartiles, and upper and lower limits. The median is $\frac{47+52}{2} = 49.5$, the lower quartile is $\frac{41+43}{2} = 42$, and the upper quartile is $\frac{60+65}{2} = 62.5$. The box of the box-and-whisker plot goes through the quartiles, and a line through the box represents the median of the data. The whiskers extend from the box to the lower and upper limits, unless there are any outliers in the set. In this case, there are no outliers, so the box-and-whisker plot in choice A correctly represents the data set.

To draw a pie chart, find the percentage of data contained in each of the ranges shown. There are 3 out of 16 numbers between 30 and 39, inclusive, so the percentage shown in the pie chart for that range of data is $\frac{3}{16} \times 100\% \approx 19\%$; there are five values between 40 and 49, inclusive, so the percentage of data for that sector is $\frac{5}{16} \times 100\% \approx 31\%$; $\frac{3}{16} \times 100\% \approx 19\%$ of the data is within the range of 50–59, and $\frac{5}{16} \times 100\% \approx 31\%$ is within the range of 60–69. The pie chart does not show the correct percentage of data in each category.

To draw a cumulative frequency histogram, find the cumulative frequency of the data.

Range	Frequency	Cumulative Frequency
30-39	3	3
40-49	5	8
50-59	3	11
60-69	5	16

The histogram does not show the correct cumulative frequency.

The data points in the line graph in choice D do not correspond to the data points given for the question.

9. A: Percent error $= \frac{|\text{actual value}-\text{measured value}|}{\text{actual value}} \times 100\%$, and the average percent error is the sum of the percent errors for each trial divided by the number of trials.

	Percent Error Trial 1	Percent Error Trial 2	Percent Error Trial 3	Percent Error Trial 4	Average Percent Error
Scale 1	0.4%	0.6%	0.2%	0.6%	0.45%
Scale 2	0.2%	0.2%	0.4%	0.2%	0.25%

The percent error for Scale 2 is less than the percent error for Scale 1, so it is more accurate. The more precise scale is also Scale 2 because its range of values, $4.99\text{ g} - 5.02\text{ g} = 0.03\text{ g}$, is smaller than Scale 1's range of values, $4.97\text{ g} - 5.03\text{ g} = 0.06\text{ g}$.

10. C: First, add the matrices in parentheses, then multiply the resulting matrices together:

$$\begin{aligned} \begin{bmatrix} 1 & -3 & 2 \end{bmatrix} \begin{bmatrix} (-3+3) \\ (2+4) \\ (1-2) \end{bmatrix} &= \begin{bmatrix} 1 & -3 & 2 \end{bmatrix} \begin{bmatrix} 0 \\ 6 \\ -1 \end{bmatrix} \\ &= [(1)(0) + (-3)(6) + (2)(-1)] \\ &= [-20] \end{aligned}$$

Note that the product of a 1×3 matrix and a 3×1 matrix, in that order, is a 1×1 matrix. If the order was reversed, the product would be a 3×3 matrix.

11. A: "A square root of twice the sum of x and 6 is equal to half of x" is represented by the equation $\sqrt{2(x+6)} = \frac{1}{2}x$. Solve for x.

$$\begin{aligned} \sqrt{2(x+6)} &= \frac{1}{2}x \\ \sqrt{2x+12} &= \frac{1}{2}x \\ \left(\sqrt{2x+12}\right)^2 &= \left(\frac{1}{2}x\right)^2 \\ 2x+12 &= \frac{1}{4}x^2 \\ 4(2x+12) &= x^2 \\ 8x+48 &= x^2 \\ x^2 - 8x - 48 &= 0 \\ (x+4)(x-12) &= 0 \\ x &= -4, 12 \end{aligned}$$

There is not an answer choice of, "no solution." So, there is no need to check your answer in the original equation. 12 must be a possible value of x.

12. B: Graphically, a relationship between x and y can be identified as a function if the graph passes the vertical line test. Choice B is the graph of $y = x^3$, which is a function because it passes the vertical line test. A function is a relationship in which for every element of the domain (x) produces exactly one element of the range (y).

The first relation is a circle, which fails the vertical line test for functions. Choice C is a parabola on its side, which also fails the vertical line test and is therefore not a function. The relation in choice D has an element of the domain (2) that maps to two different range values, so it is also not a function.

13. C: There are three ways in which two women from the same department can be selected: two women can be selected from Biology, two women can be selected from Chemistry, or two women can be selected from Physics. Since the events of choosing one woman and then another are both independent events, multiply the two probabilities together to get the probability of choosing two women from the same department.

Biology	**Chemistry**	**Physics**
$\frac{26}{129} \times \frac{25}{128} = \frac{650}{16{,}512}$	$\frac{31}{129} \times \frac{30}{128} = \frac{930}{16{,}512}$	$\frac{20}{129} \times \frac{19}{128} = \frac{380}{16{,}512}$

Since any of these is a distinct possible outcome, the probability that two women will be selected from the same department is the sum of these outcomes.

$$\frac{650}{16{,}512} + \frac{930}{16{,}512} + \frac{380}{16{,}512} = \frac{1{,}960}{16{,}512} \approx 0.119 = 11.9\%$$

14. B: If the statement is written in the form $p \rightarrow q$, then the contrapositive is represented as $\neg q \rightarrow \neg p$. Thus, the contrapositive should read, "If Bryan does not have an allergic reaction, he does not eat peanuts."

15. B: A score of 91 is one standard deviation above the mean ($84 + 7 = 91$). Since approximately 68% of the data is within one standard deviation of the mean, about 32% ($100\% - 68\%$) of the data is outside of one standard deviation within the mean. Normally distributed data is symmetric about the mean, which means that about 16% of the data lies below one standard deviation below the mean and about 16% of data lies above one standard deviation above the mean. Therefore, approximately 16% of the students scored 91 or higher. Since 16% of 250 is 40, about 40 students scored at least 91.

16. D: Consider each answer choice. The x-intercept is the point at which $f(x) = 0$. When $0 = \log_b x$, $b^0 = x$; since $b^0 = 1$, the x-intercept of $f(x) = \log_b x$ is always 1. If $f(x) = \log_b x$ and $x = b$, then $f(x) = \log_b b$, which is, by definition, 1 ($b^1 = b$). The statement $f(x) < 0$ is true only for x-values between 0 and 1. Choice D states, "If $g(x) = x^b$, the graph of $f(x)$ is symmetric to the graph of $g(x)$ with respect to $y = x$." This is a false statement. On the other hand, if $g(x) = b^x$, then $f(x)$ and $g(x)$ are inverse functions and are therefore symmetric with respect to $y = x$.

17. B: Euclidean geometry has five axioms: between any two points, a single, straight line segment may be drawn; any given right angle is congruent to any other right angle; straight line segments may be extended indefinitely; given a center point and a radius, a circle may be drawn; and if two lines are on a plane and intersected by another line, and if the internal angles on one side combine to less than two right angles, then the straight lines will eventually meet on the side where the angles combine to less than two right angles. Statement II is close to one of Euclid's axioms, but it is missing key information about being given a point and radius.

18. D: A system of linear equations can be solved by using matrices or by using the graphing, substitution, or elimination method. The elimination method is shown here.

$$\begin{cases} -4x + 3y = 8 \\ 6x - 2y = -7 \end{cases}$$

To eliminate y by the elimination method, multiply the top equation by 2 and the bottom equation by 3 so that the coefficients of the y-terms will be additive inverses.

$$\begin{aligned} 2(-4x + 3y) &= (8)2 \\ -8x + 6y &= 16 \end{aligned} \qquad \begin{aligned} 3(6x - 2y) &= (-7)(3) \\ 18x - 6y &= -21 \end{aligned}$$

Then, add the two equations and solve for x.

$$\begin{array}{rrrl} & -8x & +6y & = 16 \\ + & 18x & -6y & = -21 \\ \hline & & 10x & = -5 \\ & & x & = -\frac{1}{2} \end{array}$$

Substitute $-\frac{1}{2}$ for x in either of the given equations and solve for y.

$$\begin{aligned} -4x + 3y &= 8 \\ -4\left(-\frac{1}{2}\right) + 3y &= 8 \\ 2 + 3y &= 8 \\ 3y &= 6 \\ y &= 2 \end{aligned}$$

The solution to the system of equations is $\left(-\frac{1}{2}, 2\right)$.

19. B: The sequence $\frac{1}{5}\frac{1}{25}\frac{1}{125}\frac{1}{625}$ ... may be used to represent the situation. Substituting the initial value of $\frac{1}{5}$ and the common ratio of $\frac{1}{5}$ into the formula $S = \frac{a}{1-r}$:

$$S = \frac{\frac{1}{5}}{1 - \frac{1}{5}} = \frac{\frac{1}{5}}{\frac{4}{5}} = \frac{1}{4}$$

20. A: Since the y-coordinates of points P and Q are the same, line segment $\overline{PQ}$ is a horizontal line segment whose length is the difference in the x-coordinates a and c. Because the length of a line cannot be negative, and because it is unknown whether $a > c$ or $a < c$, $PQ = |a - c|$ or $|c - a|$. Since the x-coordinates of Q and P' are the same, line segment $\overline{P'Q}$ is a vertical line segment whose length is $|d - b|$ or $|b - d|$. The quadrilateral formed by the transformation of $\overline{PQ}$ to $\overline{P'Q'}$ is a parallelogram. If the base of the parallelogram is $\overline{PQ}$, then the height is $\overline{P'Q}$ since $\overline{PQ} \perp \overline{P'Q}$. For a parallelogram, $A = bh$, so $A = |a - c| \times |b - d|$.

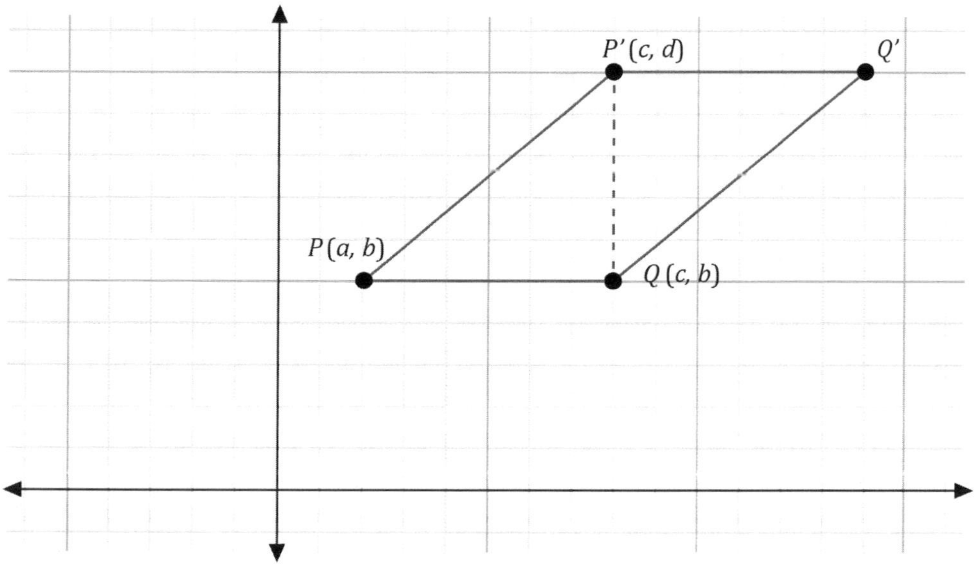

21. B: There are three ways in which two women from the same department can be selected. Two women can be selected from the first department, two women can be selected from the second department, or two women can be selected from the third department.

Department 1	**Department 2**	**Department 3**
$\frac{12}{103} \times \frac{11}{102} = \frac{132}{10{,}506}$	$\frac{28}{103} \times \frac{27}{102} = \frac{756}{10{,}506}$	$\frac{16}{103} \times \frac{15}{102} = \frac{240}{10{,}506}$

Since any of these is a distinct possible outcome, the probability that two women will be selected from the same department is the sum of these outcomes.

$$\frac{132}{10{,}506} + \frac{756}{10{,}506} + \frac{240}{10{,}506} = \frac{1{,}128}{10{,}506} \approx 0.107$$

Converting this to a percentage, the probability that two women from the same department will be chosen is approximately 10.7%.

22. C: The interior angles of a trapezoid add up to 360°. The two larger angles on each trapezoid are congruent and are equal to $x - 24°$. The other two angles add up to x, as shown on the far right. So, $x - 24 + x - 24 + x = 360$. Solve for x:

$$\begin{aligned} x - 24 + x - 24 + x &= 360 \\ 3x - 48 &= 360 \\ 3x &= 408 \\ x &= 136° \end{aligned}$$

23. B: The ratio of revenue of new car sales to used car sales is 3 : 5. This means that the total revenue of cars sold (both new and used) is $3 + 5 = 8$. The used car sales are $\frac{5}{8}$ of the total sales:

$$\frac{5}{8} \times \$287{,}400 = \$179{,}625$$

24. D: To solve this equation, start by squaring both sides, then isolate the variable.

$$2 - \sqrt{x} = \sqrt{x - 20}$$
$$\left(2 - \sqrt{x}\right)^2 = \left(\sqrt{x - 20}\right)^2$$
$$\left(2 - \sqrt{x}\right)\left(2 - \sqrt{x}\right) = x - 20$$
$$4 - 4\sqrt{x} + x = x - 20$$
$$-4\sqrt{x} = -24$$
$$\sqrt{x} = 6$$
$$x = 36$$

When solving radical equations, check for extraneous solutions by substituting the found value into the original equation.

$$2 - \sqrt{x} = \sqrt{x - 20}$$
$$2 - \sqrt{36} = \sqrt{36 - 20}$$
$$2 - 6 = \sqrt{16}$$
$$-4 \neq 4$$

Since the solution results in an untrue statement, there is no solution. Alternatively, consider the graphs of the left and right side of the given equation. Notice the graphs $y = 2 - \sqrt{x}$ and $y = \sqrt{x - 20}$ do not intersect, which confirms there is no solution.

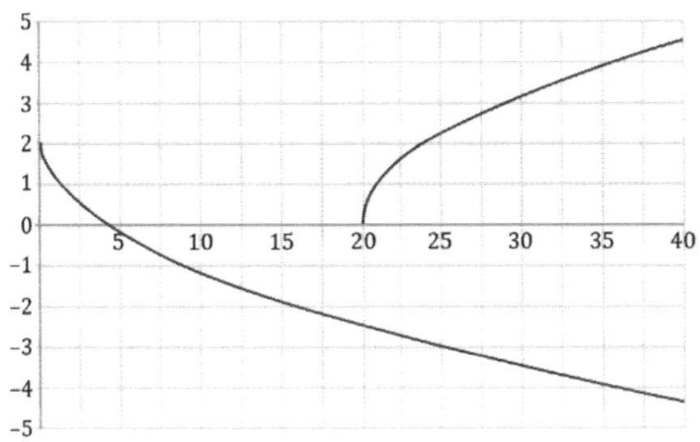

25. D: Since there are 100 cm in a meter, on a 1 : 100 scale drawing, each centimeter represents one meter. Therefore, an area of one square centimeter on the drawing represents one square meter in actuality. Since the area of the room in the scale drawing is 30 cm^2, the room's actual area is 30 m^2.

Another way to determine the area of the room is to write and solve an equation, such as this one: $\frac{l}{100} \times \frac{w}{100} = 30\ \text{cm}^2$, where l and w are the dimensions of the actual room.

$$\frac{lw}{10{,}000} = 30\ \text{cm}^2$$
$$\text{Area} = 300{,}000\ \text{cm}^2$$

Since this is not one of the answer choices, convert cm^2 to m^2.

$$300{,}000\ \text{cm}^2 \times \frac{1\ \text{m}}{100\ \text{cm}} \times \frac{1\ \text{m}}{100\ \text{cm}} = 30\ \text{m}^2$$

26. C: Nominal data are data that are collected which have no intrinsic quantity or order. For instance, a survey might ask the respondent to identify his or her gender. While it is possible to compare the relative frequency of each response (for example, "most of the respondents are women"), it is not possible to calculate the mean, which requires data to be numeric, or median, which requires data to be ordered. Interval data are both numeric and ordered, so mean and median can be determined, as can the mode, the interval within which there are the most data. Ordinal data has an inherent order, but there is not a set interval between two points. For example, a survey might ask whether the respondent whether he or she was very dissatisfied, dissatisfied, neutral, satisfied, or very satisfied with the customer service received. Since the data are not numeric, the mean cannot be calculated, but since ordering the data is possible, the median has context.

27. B: One way to approach this problem is to first consider the number of arrangements of the five members of the family if Tasha (T) and Mac (M) must sit together. Treat them as a unit seated in a fixed location at the table; then arrange the other three family members (A, B, and C):

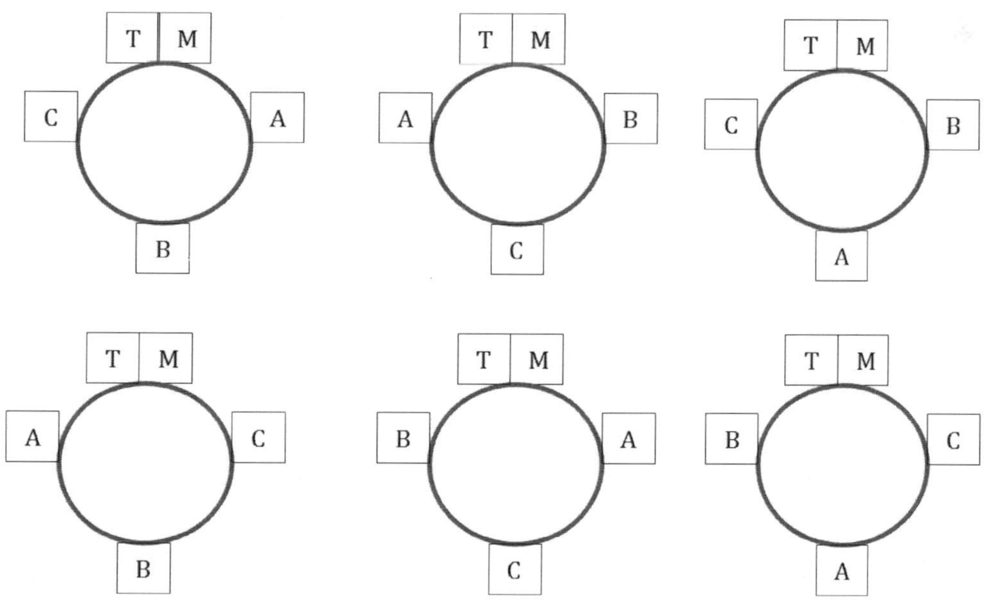

There are six ways to arrange four units around a circle as shown. Any other arrangement would be a rotation in which the elements are in the same order and would therefore not be a unique arrangement. Of course, Mac and Tasha are not actually a single unit. They would still be sitting beside each other if they were to trade seats, so there are 12 arrangements in which the two are seated next to one another. In all other arrangements of the five family members, they are separated. Therefore, to find the number of arrangements in which Tasha and Mac are *not* sitting together, subtract 12 from the possible arrangement of five units around a circle. There are $(n-1)!$ ways to arrange n units around a circle for $n > 1$. So, $(5-1)! - 12 = 24 - 12 = 12$.

28. A: The set of whole numbers, $\{0, 1, 2, 3, \ldots\}$, does not contain the number –4. Since –4 is an integer, it is also a rational number and a real number.

29. C: The period of the pendulum is a function of the square root of the length of its string, and is independent of the mass of the pendulum or the angle from which it is released. If the period of Pendulum 1's swing is four times the period of Pendulum 2's swing, then the length of Pendulum 1's string must be 16 times the length of Pendulum 2's swing since all other values besides L in the expression $2\pi\sqrt{\frac{L}{g}}$ remain the same.

30. C: The expression representing the charge for Ride Service A is $\$10 + \$0.25(m-10)$, where m is the number of miles. Set this expression equal to the charge for Ride Service B, which is $\$0.40m$. Solve for m to find the number of miles the two companies charge the same amount.

$$\begin{aligned} \$10 + \$0.25(m-10) &= \$0.40m \\ \$10 + \$0.25m - \$2.50 &= \$0.40m \\ \$7.50 &= \$0.15m \\ m &= 50 \end{aligned}$$

So, the cost of the two services would be the same for a 50-mile ride.

31. 461: The Law of Sines is $\frac{\sin A}{a} = \frac{\sin B}{b} = \frac{\sin C}{c}$, but to solve this problem we only need $\frac{\sin A}{a} = \frac{\sin B}{b}$. By substitution, that equation becomes $\frac{\sin 92^\circ}{1{,}180} = \frac{\sin 23^\circ}{x}$. Solving for x, the equation results in $x = \frac{1{,}180 \sin 23^\circ}{\sin 92^\circ} = 461.3$ feet. Rounded to the nearest foot, this is 461 feet.

32. C: To find the volume of square pyramid use the formula $A = \frac{1}{3}lwh$, where l is the length of the base, w is the width of the base, and h is the height of the pyramid. The volume of the greenhouse is $\frac{x^2y}{3}$. If the height were increased by 4 ft, the volume would be $\frac{x^2(y+4)}{3} = \frac{x^2y+4x^2}{3}$. Notice this is the volume of the greenhouse, $\frac{x^2y}{3}$, increased by $\frac{4x^2}{3}$.

33. B: The graph of $f(x)$ is stretched vertically by a factor of 4 with respect to $y = \sin x$, so $a_1 = 4$. The graph of $g(x)$ is stretched vertically by a factor of 2 and is inverted with respect to the graph of $y = \cos x$, so $a_2 = -2$. Therefore, the statement $a_2 < 0 < a_1$ is true.

34. D: First, apply the laws of exponents to simplify the expression on the left. Then, add the two fractions.

$\frac{(x^2y^{-3})(4xy)^2}{16x^4y^4} + \frac{3}{2xy}$	Write out the original expression.
$\frac{(x^2y^{-3})(16x^2y^2)}{16x^4y^4} + \frac{3}{2xy}$	Simplify the squared term in the left fraction's numerator.

$\frac{16x^4y^{-1}}{16x^4y^4} + \frac{3}{2xy}$	Multiply the two monomials in the left fraction's numerator using the exponent rule $x^m \cdot x^n = x^{m+n}$.
$\frac{1}{y^5} + \frac{3}{2xy}$	Simplify the left fraction using the exponent rule $\frac{x^m}{x^n} = x^{m-n}$ and the rule $x^{-n} = \frac{1}{x^n}$.
$\frac{1}{y^5} \cdot \frac{2x}{2x} + \frac{3}{2xy} \cdot \frac{y^4}{y^4}$	Create common denominators between the two fractions by multiplying them each by a factor of 1.
$\frac{2x}{2xy^5} + \frac{3y^4}{2xy^5}$	Simplify the multiplication.
$\frac{2x + 3y^4}{2xy^5}$	Add the two fractions.

35. A: One way to determine which is the graph of $f(x) = -3|-x + 2| + 1$ is to find $f(x)$ for a few values of x. For example, when $x = 0$, $f(0) = -3|0 + 2| + 1 = -5$. Graphs A and C pass through $(0, -5)$, but graphs B and D do not. When $x = 2$, $f(2) = -3|-2 + 2| + 1 = 1$. Graph A passes through $(2,1)$, but graph C does not. Graph A is the correct graph.

36. D: Radioactive decay can be modeled with an exponential function. The path of a sound wave is modeled by a sine or cosine function. The path of a ball being kicked into the air is modeled by a quadratic function. The distance an object travels over time when the rate is constant is modeled by a linear function.

37. A: First, use the table of values to write polynomial equations for $f(x)$ and $g(x)$: $f(x) = 3x^2$ and $g(x) = 2x - 2$. Then, use those equations to find $f(g(-3))$.

$$g(-3) = 2(-3) - 2 = -8$$
$$f(-8) = 3(-8)^2 = 192$$

So, $f(g(-3)) = 192$.

38. B: A cube has six square faces. The arrangement of these faces in a two-dimensional figure is a net of a cube if the figure can be folded to form a cube. If choice B is folded, the bottom square in the second column will overlap the fourth square in the top row, so the figure does not represent a net of a cube. The other figures represent three of the eleven possible nets of a cube.

39. C: The Babylonians used a base-60 numeral system, which is still used in the division of an hour into 60 minutes, a minute into 60 seconds, and a circle into 360 degrees. The word "algebra" and its development as a discipline separate from geometry are attributed to the Arabic/Islamic civilization. The Greek philosopher Thales is credited with using deductive reasoning to prove geometric concepts. Boolean logic was introduced by British mathematician George Boole.

40. B: If $f(x) = 10^x$ and $f(x) = 1$, then $1 = 10^x$. Any number to a power of 0 equals 1, so $10^0 = 1$ and $x = 0$.

41. C: The approximate price of the fence is found by rounding to 70 feet at \$4 per foot.

$$\text{Price} = 70 \text{ ft} \times \$4/\text{ft} = \$280$$

Therefore, he will spend approximately \$280 on fencing. The actual price is 71 ft × \$3.98/ft = \$282.58.

42. A: The period of the unmodified tangent function $y = tan(x)$ is simply π. However, when the x is multiplied by a coefficient $b \neq 1$, the function is compressed or stretched horizontally, changing its period to $\frac{\pi}{|b|}$. Here, $b = 2$, so the new period is $\frac{\pi}{2}$. (The "+6" in the given equation shifts the function horizontally but has no effect on the period.)

43. B: In this sequence, each term is double the previous term. For example, $7 \times 2 = 14$, and $14 \times 2 = 28$. The next term must be $56 \times 2 = 112$.

44. B: In this sequence, 5 and 4 are added alternatively to successive numbers to determine the next numeral: $54 + 5 = 59, 59 + 4 = 63$, etc. Since $68 + 4 = 72$, the next element is calculated by adding 5: $72 + 5 = 77$, so 77 is the next term in the sequence.

45. B: First, use the properties of logarithms to solve for y:

$2\log_4 y + \log_4 16 = 3$	Write out the original equation.
$\log_4 y^2 + \log_4 16 = 3$	Use the power rule for logarithms: $\log_b(x^a) = a \cdot \log_b x$.
$\log_4 16y^2 = 3$	Then, use the product rule for logarithms: $\log_b x + \log_b y = \log_b(xy)$.
$16y^2 = 4^3$	Next, convert the logarithm to an exponential expression.
$16y^2 = 64$	Simplify the right side.
$y^2 = 4$	Divide both sides by 16.
$y = 2$	Take the positive square root of both sides.

Finally, substitute 2 for y in the expression $\log_y 256$ and simplify: $\log_2 256 = 8$ since $2^8 = 256$.

46. B: The equation of the circle is given in general form. When the equation is written in the standard form $(x - h)^2 + (y - k)^2 = r^2$, where (h, k) is the center of the circle and r is the radius of the circle, the radius is easy to determine. Putting the equation into standard form requires completing the square for x and y.

$$x^2 + y^2 - 4x + 6y = 5$$
$$(x^2 - 4x + 4) + (y^2 + 6y + 9) = 5 + 4 + 9$$
$$(x - 2)^2 + (y + 3)^2 = 18$$

Since $r^2 = 18$, and since r must be a positive number, $r = \sqrt{18} = 3\sqrt{2}$.

47. B: A quick estimate of the total miles can be obtained by rounding each leg of the trip to the nearest whole mile and finding the sum: $5 + 7 + 14 + 15 = 41$ miles.

48. B: Determine the probability of each choice.

For choice A, this is the total number of students in the broccoli circle of the Venn diagram divided by the total number of students surveyed:

$$\frac{10+4+3+15}{90} = \frac{32}{90} \approx 35.6\%$$

For choice B, this is the total number of students in the carrots circle and also in at least one other circle divided by the total number in the carrots circle:

$$\frac{15+3+6}{15+3+6+27} = \frac{24}{51} \approx 47.1\%$$

For choice C, this is the number of students in the intersection of all three circles divided by the total number in the overlap of the broccoli and cauliflower circles:

$$\frac{3}{3+4} = \frac{3}{7} \approx 42.9\%$$

For choice D, this is the number of students outside of all the circles divided by the total number of students surveyed:

$$\frac{23}{90} \approx 25.6\%$$

Since choice B has the highest percentage, it is the choice that is most probable.

49. A: Sketch a diagram and label the known segments (figure not drawn to scale).

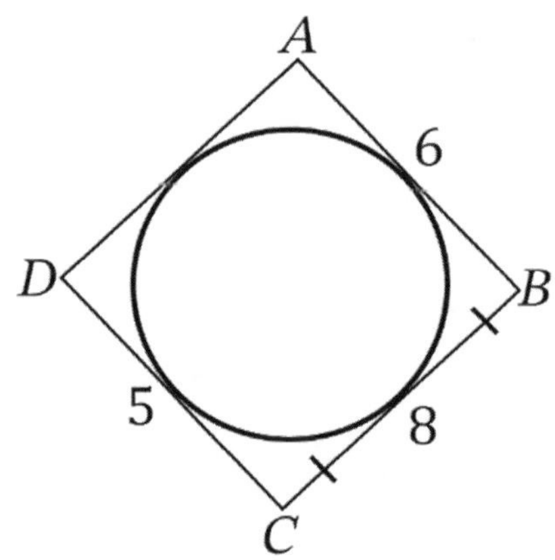

Use the property that two segments are congruent when they originate from the same point outside of a circle and are tangent to the circle. The point of tangency of $\overline{CB}$ divides the segment into two pieces measuring 4 and 4; the point of tangency of $\overline{BA}$ divides the segment into two pieces measuring 4 and 2; the point of tangency of $\overline{CD}$ divides the segment into two pieces measuring 4 and 1; the point of tangency of $\overline{AD}$ divides the segment into two pieces measuring 2 and 1. Therefore, $\overline{AD} = 2 + 1 = 3$.

50. C: In Class 1, 27 students submitted late work, so the median is between the 13th and 14th piece of homework. Both the 13th and 14th fall on Day 4, so the median for Class 1 is 4. In Class 2, 23 students submitted late work, so the median is at the 12th piece of homework. This falls on Day 7. So, because $7 - 4 = 3$, the median number of days late in Class 1 is 3 less than the median number of days late in Class 2.

To find the mean late time for each class, find the sum of the late times and divide by the number of students turning in late work in each class. If the frequency of a one-day late time is 4, the number 1 is added four times (1×4), if frequency of a two-day late time is 5, the number 2 is added five times (2×5), and so on. So, to find the average turn-in time, divide the sum of the products of each late time and its corresponding frequency by the number of late turn-ins in each class. For Class 1, the mean late time is 5.22 days, which rounds to approximately 5 days.

$$\text{Mean} = \frac{4(1) + 5(2) + 3(3) + 2(4) + 3(5) + 1(6) + 1(7) + 2(9) + 4(10) + 2(12)}{4 + 5 + 3 + 2 + 3 + 1 + 1 + 2 + 4 + 2} = \frac{141}{27} \approx 5.22$$

For Class 2, the mean late time is 6.57, which rounds to approximately 7 days.

$$\text{Mean} = \frac{1(1) + 2(2) + 2(3) + 1(4) + 4(6) + 5(7) + 3(8) + 1(9) + 2(10) + 2(12)}{1 + 2 + 2 + 1 + 4 + 5 + 3 + 1 + 2 + 2} = \frac{151}{23} \approx 6.57$$

So, because $7 - 5 = 2$, the students in Class 2 turned in work 2 days later than in Class 1.

The mode late time is the date for which the frequency is the highest. For Class 1, the mode late time is 2 days, and for Class 2, the mode late time is 7 days.

The median late time for Class 1 is 4 and the mean is 4.96, so the median late time is less than the mean.

51. D: Levi walked 3 miles from home and then back again, so he walked a total of 6 miles. Therefore, statement III is true. He traveled these 6 miles in 6 hours, so his average speed was 1 mph. Therefore, statement I is true. He walked 3 miles from point A to B in 1 hour and 2 miles from E to F in 1 hour, so his speed averaged 3 mph between A and B and 2 mph between E and F. Therefore, statement II is false.

52. D: Let b represent the base of the triangle. The height h of the triangle is the altitude drawn from the vertex opposite of b to side b.

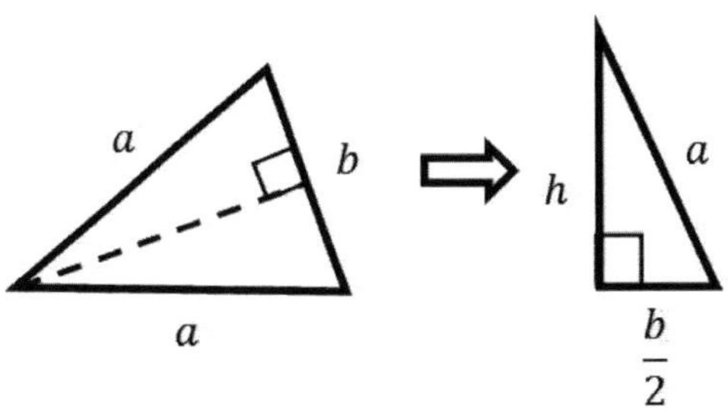

The height of the triangle can be found in terms of a and b by using the Pythagorean theorem.

$$h^2 + \left(\frac{b}{2}\right)^2 = a^2$$

$$h = \sqrt{a^2 - \frac{b^2}{4}}$$

$$h = \sqrt{\frac{4a^2 - b^2}{4}}$$

$$h = \frac{\sqrt{4a^2 - b^2}}{2}$$

The area of a triangle is $A = \frac{1}{2}bh$, so $A = \frac{1}{2}b\left(\frac{\sqrt{4a^2-b^2}}{2}\right) = \frac{b\sqrt{4a^2-b^2}}{4}$.

53. B: The path of a bullet is a parabola, which is the graph of a quadratic function. The path of a sound wave can be modeled by a sine or cosine function. The distance an object travels over time given a constant rate is a linear relationship, while radioactive decay is modeled by an exponential function.

54. B: If the statement is written in the form $p \to q$, then the converse is represented as $q \to p$. Thus, the converse should read, "If it is winter, then I go skiing."

55. B: To find the second derivative of the function, take the derivative of the first derivative of the function. Remember, to take a derivative, multiply the exponent of each term by the term's coefficient and then decrease the exponent by 1.

$$f(x) = -3x^3 - x^2 + 2x - 4$$
$$f'(x) = -9x^2 - 2x + 2$$
$$f''(x) = -18x - 2$$

56. A: The revenue Jen receives from each method of sale is:

$0.8 \times 0.75 \times \$10.50 = \$6.30$ from Store A
$0.8(\$11.00 - \$1.50) = \$7.60$ from Store B
$\$6.75 + \$2.50 - \$2.50 = \$6.75$ from Store C

So, Store A will give the lowest revenue, Store C is next, and Store B brings the highest revenue during the sale.

57. B: First, simplify the expression by expanding the squared binomial.

$$(4 - i)^2 - (2 - 4i)$$
$$(4 - i)(4 - i) - (2 - 4i)$$
$$(16 - 8i + i^2) - (2 - 4i)$$

Then, distribute the negative sign and combine like terms.

$$16 - 8i + i^2 - 2 + 4i$$
$$14 - 4i + i^2$$

Remember, $i^2 = -1$, so substitute this value into the expression and combine like terms once more.

$$14 - 4i - 1$$
$$13 - 4i$$

58. B: The population is approximately 36,000, so one-quarter of the population consists of about 9,000 individuals under age 35. A third of 9,000 is 3,000, which is the approximate number of students in grades K–12. Since there are thirteen grades, divide 3,000 by 13. There are about 230 students in each grade. So, the number of fourth graders is between 200 and 300.

59. A: The equation for this scenario is $2b + 3c \geq 150$, where b is the number of brownies that must be sold and c is the number of cupcakes that must be sold. Solve for the intercepts of the inequality by momentarily changing the inequality sign to an equal sign, substituting 0 for b and solving for c, and then substituting 0 for c and solving for b. The intercepts of this linear inequality are $b = 75$ and $c = 50$. The x-axis represents the number of brownies sold, so the x-intercept is $(75, 0)$. The y-axis represents the number of cupcakes sold, so the y-intercept is $(0, 50)$. The solid line through the two intercepts, (75,0) and (0,50), represents the minimum number of each type of baked good that must be sold to offset production costs. Since you are breaking even or making a profit, shade above the line.

60. C: The center of the sphere is shared by the center of the cube, and each of the corners of the cube touches the surface of the sphere. Therefore, the diameter of the sphere is the line that passes through the center of the cube and connects one corner of the cube to the opposite corner. In the illustration below, notice that the diameter d of the sphere can be represented as the hypotenuse of a right triangle with a short leg measuring 4 units. (Since the volume of the cube is 64 cubic units, each of its sides measures $\sqrt[3]{64} = 4$ units.) The long leg of the triangle is the diagonal of the base of the cube.

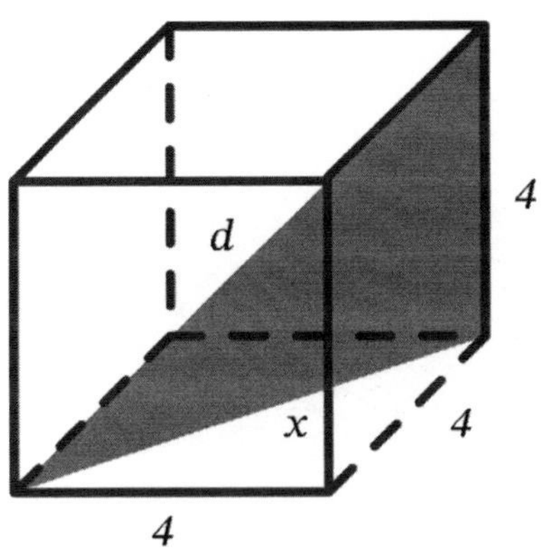

The length of the long leg can be found using the Pythagorean theorem:

$$x^2 = 4^2 + 4^2 = 32$$
$$x = \sqrt{32} = 4\sqrt{2}$$

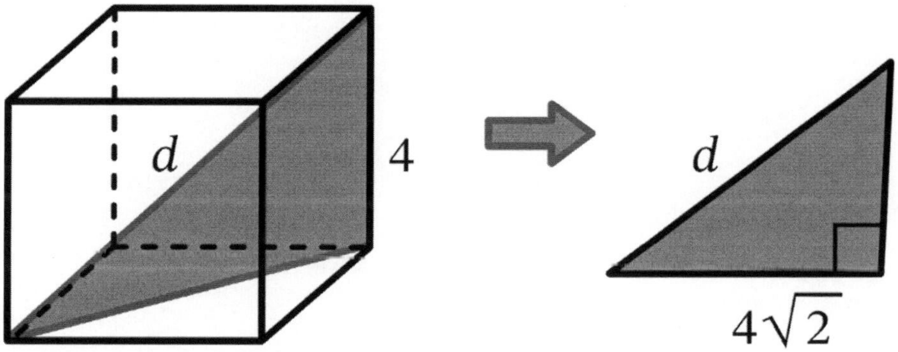

Use the Pythagorean theorem again to find d, the diameter of the sphere:

$$d^2 = (4\sqrt{2})^2 + 4^2 = 32 + 16 = 48$$
$$d = \sqrt{48} = 4\sqrt{3}$$

To find the volume of the sphere, use the formula $V = \frac{4}{3}\pi r^3$. Since the radius r of the sphere is half the diameter, $r = 2\sqrt{3}$, and $V = \frac{4}{3}\pi(2\sqrt{3})^3 = \frac{4}{3}\pi(24\sqrt{3}) = 32\pi\sqrt{3}$ cubic units.

61. C: There are 6 occurrences of aa, so the experimental probability of getting genotype aa is $\frac{6}{500} = 0.012$. There are 21 occurrences of bb, so the experimental probability of getting genotype bb is $\frac{21}{500} = 0.042$. The experimental probability of either getting genotype aa or bb is $0.012 + 0.042 = 0.054$. Multiply this experimental probability by 100,000 to find the number of individuals expected to be homozygous for either allele in a population of 100,000: $0.054 \times 100{,}000 = 5{,}400$.

62. D: Determine the probability of each option (if s = likes baseball, b = likes basketball, and f = likes football).

For choice A, this is the total number of students in the football circle of the Venn diagram divided by the total number of students surveyed:

$$P(f) = \frac{47 + 22 + 19 + 31}{241} = \frac{119}{241} \approx 49.4\%$$

For choice B, this is the total number of students in the baseball circle and also in at least one other circle divided by the total number in the baseball circle:

$$P(s \cup f|b) = \frac{28 + 19 + 22}{28 + 19 + 22 + 34} = \frac{69}{103} \approx 67.0\%$$

For choice C, this is the number of students in the intersection of all three circles divided by the total number in the overlap of the baseball and basketball circles:

$$P(s|b \cap f) = \frac{19}{19 + 28} = \frac{19}{47} \approx 40.4\%$$

For choice D, this is the number of students outside of all the circles divided by the total number of students surveyed:

$$P([c \cup b \cup f]') = \frac{18}{241} \approx 7.5\%$$

Since Choice D has the lowest probability, it is the correct answer.

63. B: A test of each option at $x = -3$, $x = 0$, and $x = 4$ demonstrates that choice B is the closest representation.

x	**Observed**	y_a	y_b	y_c	y_d
-3	$\sim\frac{3}{4}$	$\frac{1}{3}$	$\frac{2}{3}$	$-\frac{7}{3}$	$\frac{1}{9}$
0	$\sim -\frac{3}{4}$	$-\frac{2}{3}$	$-\frac{2}{3}$	$\frac{1}{3}$	$-\frac{4}{3}$
4	$\sim\frac{3}{4}$	2	$\frac{2}{3}$	$\frac{7}{3}$	$\frac{8}{9}$

64. A: First, multiply the numerator and denominator by the denominator's conjugate, $3 + 2i$. Then, simplify the result and write the answer in the form $a + bi$. Recall, $i^2 = -1$.

$$\begin{aligned} \frac{4+i}{3-2i} \times \frac{3+2i}{3+2i} &= \frac{12 + 8i + 3i + 2i^2}{9 - 4i^2} \\ &= \frac{12 + 11i - 2}{9 + 4} \\ &= \frac{10 + 11i}{13} \\ &= \frac{10}{13} + \frac{11}{13}i \end{aligned}$$

65. A: The x-intercept is the point at which $f(x) = 0$. When $0 = \log_b x$, $b^0 = x$; since $b^0 = 1$, the x-intercept of $f(x) = \log_b x$ is always 1. If $f(x) = \log_b x$ and $x = b$, then $f(x) = \log_b b$, which is, by definition, 1 ($b^1 = b$). The statement $f(x) < 0$ is true only for x-values between 0 and 1($0 < x < 1$). If $g(x) = b^x$, then $f(x)$ and $g(x)$ are inverse functions and are therefore symmetric with respect to $y = x$.

66. B: The set of rational numbers includes every number that can be written as quotient of two integers. Since $\sqrt{32}$ cannot be expressed as a fraction of integers, it is not a rational number, but it does fit in the sets of real and complex numbers.

67. C: Sketch a diagram (this one is not to scale) and label the known segments. Because $\overline{CD}$ is bisected, the point of tangency divides the segment into two pieces measuring 4 and 4. From here, use the property that two segments are congruent when they originate from the same point outside of a circle and are both tangent to the circle. The point of tangency of $\overline{BC}$ divides the segment into two pieces measuring 4 and 6; the point of tangency of $\overline{AB}$ divides the segment into two pieces measuring 6 and 8; the point of tangency of $\overline{AD}$ divides the segment into two pieces measuring 8 and 4. Therefore $\overline{AD} = 8 + 4 = 12$.

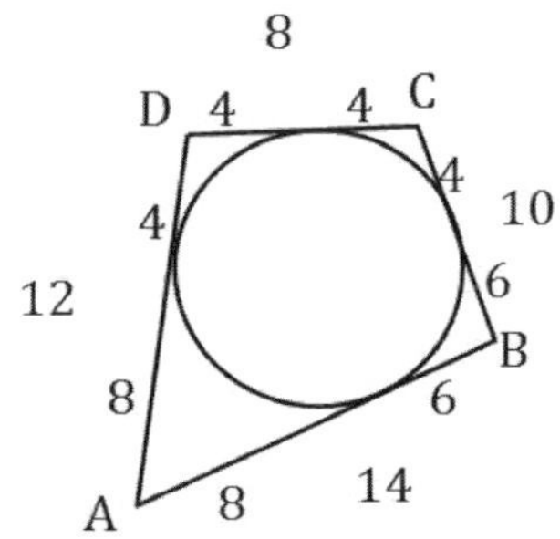

68. D: The first function shifts the graph of $y = \frac{1}{x}$ to the right one unit and down two units. The domain and range of $y = \frac{1}{x}$ are $\{x: x \neq 0\}$ and $\{y: y \neq 0\}$, so the domain and range of $y = \frac{1}{x-1} - 2$ are $\{x: x \neq 1\}$ and $\{y: y \neq -2\}$. The element –2 is not in its range.

The second function shifts the graph of $y = \sqrt{x}$ to the right one unit and up four units. The domain and range of $y = \sqrt{x}$ are $\{x: x \geq 0\}$ and $\{y: y \geq 0\}$, so the domain and range of $y = \frac{\sqrt{x-1}}{4} + 4$ are $\{x: x \geq 1\}$ and $\{y: y \geq 4\}$. The domain does not contain the element –1, and the range does not contain the element –2.

The third function shifts the graph of $y = |x|$ to the right one unit and down one unit. The domain of $y = |x|$ is the set of all real numbers and range is $\{y: y \geq 0\}$, so the domain of $y = |x - 1| - 1$ is the set of all real numbers and the range is $\{y: y \geq -1\}$. The range does not contain the element –2.

The domain of the piecewise function is the set of all real numbers. The range can be found by looking at the equations of the two lines in the piecewise function. When $x < -1$, the graph is an increasing line. When $x \geq -1$, the graph is a decreasing line. Therefore, the domain will be any y-value less than the value of the function when $x = -1$. When $x = -1, y = -(-1) + 1 = 2$.

Therefore, the domain is $y \leq 2$. The domain contains the element –1 and the range contains the element –2.

69. C: When solving radical equations, check for extraneous solutions.

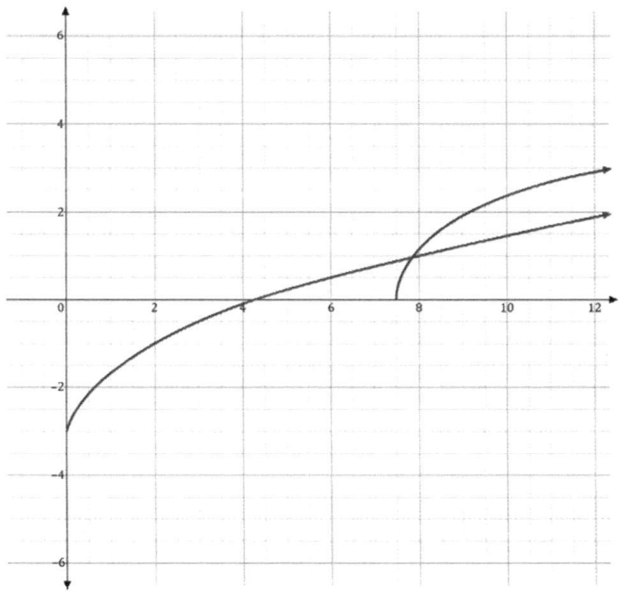

$$\sqrt{2x} - 3 = \sqrt{2x - 15}$$
$$\left(\sqrt{2x} - 3\right)^2 = \left(\sqrt{2x - 15}\right)^2$$
$$2x - 6\sqrt{2x} + 9 = 2x - 15$$
$$-6\sqrt{2x} + 9 = -15$$
$$-6\sqrt{2x} = -24$$
$$\sqrt{2x} = 4$$
$$2x = 16$$
$$x = 8$$

Check:
$$\sqrt{2(8)} - 3 = \sqrt{2(8) - 15}$$
$$\sqrt{16} - 3 = \sqrt{16 - 15}$$
$$4 - 3 = \sqrt{1}$$
$$1 = 1$$

Since the solution checks, it is a valid solution. Notice that the graphs $y = \sqrt{2x} - 3$ and $y = \sqrt{2x - 15}$ intersect, which confirms there is a solution.

70. A: We can sketch a diagram of the password to be filled in:

_ _ _ _ _

The first three characters are letters, which can repeat. Thus, there are 26 options for the first character, 26 for the second, and 26 for the third:

26 26 26 _ _

There are five even digits, so we can place a 5 in the first remaining slot. Because the digits must be unique, there are now four possibilities for the final slot:

26 26 26 5 4

Finally, we multiply the five numbers together to find the number of possible passwords:

$$26 \times 26 \times 26 \times 5 \times 4 = 351{,}520$$

71. C: When rolling two dice, there is only one way to roll a sum of 2 (rolling a 1 on each die) and 12 (rolling 6 on each die). In contrast, there are two ways to obtain a sum of 3 (rolling a 2 and 1 or a 1 and 2) and 11 (rolling a 5 and 6 or a 6 and 5), three ways to obtain a sum of 4 (1 and 3; 2 and 2; 3 and 1) or 10 (4 and 6; 5 and 5; 6 and 4), and so on. Since the probability of obtaining each sum is inconsistent, this is not a random selection.

72. C: Since a and b are multiples of 3, each can be expressed as the product of 3 and an integer. So, if we write $a = 3x$ and $b = 3y$, then the equation becomes $4(3x)^2 + (3y)^3 = c$.

$$4(3x)^2 + (3y)^3 = c$$
$$36x^2 + 27y^3 = c$$
$$9(4x^2 + 3y^3) = c$$

Since c is the product of 9 and some other integer, 9 must be a factor of c.

73. C: When a figure is reflected twice over non-parallel lines, the resulting transformation is a rotation about the point of intersection of the two lines of reflection. The two lines of reflection $y = -x + 1$ and $x = 0$ intersect at $(0,1)$. So, $\Delta A''B''C''$ represents a rotation of ΔABC about the point $(0,1)$. The angle of rotation is equal to twice the angle between the two lines of reflection when measured in a counterclockwise direction from the first to the second line of reflection. Since the angle between the lines or reflection measures 135°, the angle of rotation which is the composition of the two reflections measures 270°.

74. A: Since the figures are similar, the following proportion may be written and solved for x: $\frac{8}{6} = \frac{6}{x}$. Thus, $x = \frac{36}{8}$ or $4\frac{1}{2}$.

75. C: The graph shown is the negative exponential function $y = 2^{-x}$. Notice that the graph passes through $(-1,2)$ and $(0,1)$. A quick check of each choice demonstrates the fit:

x	x^2	$\sqrt{x}$	2^{-x}	$\log_2 x$
–1	1	undefined in $\mathbb{R}$	2	undefined
0	0	0	1	undefined

76. B: One possibility for the cross section connecting the two points across the cylinder is an ellipse.

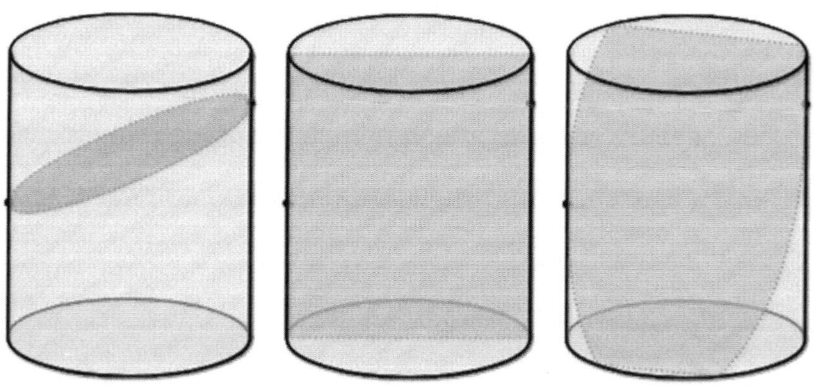

77. C: The length of the fence is equal to the perimeter of the rectangular property. The perimeter of the property is equal to the sum of twice the length and twice the width. The length is approximately 400 feet, and the width is approximately 300 feet, so the perimeter is $2(400) + 2(300) = 1{,}400$ feet.

78. C: Find the missing angle measures in the diagram by using angle and triangle properties. Then, use the law of sines to find the distance y between the window and the wife's car: $\frac{60}{\sin 15°} = \frac{y}{\sin 45°}$, so $y = \frac{60 \sin 45°}{\sin 15°} \approx 163.9$ ft. Use this number in a sine or cosine function to find x: $\sin 30° \approx \frac{x}{163.9}$, so

$x \approx 163.9 \sin 30° \approx 82$. Therefore, the man's wife is parked approximately 82 feet from the building.

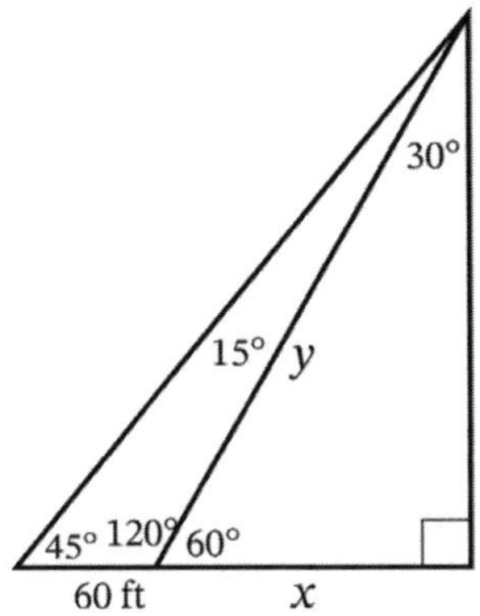

Alternatively, notice that when the man is looking down at a 45-degree angle, the triangle that is formed is an isosceles triangle, meaning that the height of his office is the same as the distance from the office to his car, or $x + 60$ feet. With this knowledge, the problem can be modeled with a single equation.

$$\frac{x+60}{x} = \tan 60°$$
$$x + 60 = x \tan 60°$$
$$60 = x \tan 60° - x$$
$$60 = x(\tan 60° - 1)$$
$$\frac{60}{\tan 60° - 1} = x$$
$$82 \approx x$$

With both methods of solving, the wife's car is approximately 82 feet from the building.

79. D: On the unit circle, $\sin\theta = \frac{1}{2}$ when $\theta = \frac{\pi}{6}$ and when $\theta = \frac{5\pi}{6}$. Since only $\frac{5\pi}{6}$ satisfies the condition $\frac{\pi}{2} < \theta < \pi$, this means that $\theta = \frac{5\pi}{6}$.

80. B: In the range $(-\infty, -2)$, the graph represented is $y = -x + 1$. In the range $[-2,1)$, the graph is a form of the greatest integer function, shifted one space to the left, $y = [\![x + 1]\!]$. In the range $[1, \infty)$, the graph is $y = -x + 3$.

81. D: There are three possibilities for being homozygous: aa, bb, or cc. We add the numbers for each of these and divide by 1,000 to find the probability that a person in this group is homozygous for one of the alleles:

$$\frac{136 + 213 + 180}{1{,}000} = \frac{529}{1{,}000} = 0.529$$

Multiply this experimental probability by 10,000 to find the number of individuals expected to be homozygous for any of the alleles in a population of 10,000: $0.529 \times 10{,}000 = 5{,}290$.

82. D: The degree of $f(x)$ is 1, the degree of $g(x)$ is 2, and the degree of $h(x)$ is 3. The leading coefficient for each function is 2. Functions $f(x)$ and $h(x)$ have exactly one real zero ($x = 1$), while $g(x)$ has two real zeros ($x = \pm 1$):

$$\begin{aligned} f(x) &= 0 \\ 2x - 2 &= 0 \\ 2x &= 2 \\ x &= 1 \end{aligned} \qquad \begin{aligned} g(x) &= 0 \\ 2x^2 - 2 &= 0 \\ 2x^2 &= 2 \\ x^2 &= 1 \\ x = 1; x &= -1 \end{aligned} \qquad \begin{aligned} h(x) &= 0 \\ 2x^3 - 2 &= 0 \\ 2x^3 &= 2 \\ x^3 &= 1 \\ x &= 1 \end{aligned}$$

83. B: First, set the equation equal to zero, then factor it.

$$\begin{aligned} 4x^3y^2 - 16x^2y &= -16x^3y + 4x^2y^2 \\ 4x^3y^2 + 16x^3y - 4x^2y^2 - 16x^2y &= 0 \\ 4x^2y(xy + 4x - y - 4) &= 0 \\ 4x^2y[x(y + 4) - 1(y + 4)] &= 0 \\ 4x^2y[(y + 4)(x - 1)] &= 0 \end{aligned}$$

Use the zero-product property to find the solution. Since the question only asks to solve for x, only look at the terms that have x in them.

$$\begin{aligned} 4x^2y &= 0 \\ x &= 0 \end{aligned} \qquad \begin{aligned} x - 1 &= 0 \\ x &= 1 \end{aligned}$$

So, the solutions are $x = \{0,1\}$.

84. D: To solve the equation, write $x^4 + 9 = 10x^2$ in quadratic form:

$$x^4 - 10x^2 + 9 = 0$$

This trinomial can be factored as $(x^2 - 1)(x^2 - 9) = 0$. Each set of parentheses contains a difference of squares, which can be factored further as $(x + 1)(x - 1)(x + 3)(x - 3) = 0$. Use the zero-product property to find the solutions to the equation.

$$\begin{aligned} x + 1 &= 0 \\ x &= -1 \end{aligned} \qquad \begin{aligned} x - 1 &= 0 \\ x &= 1 \end{aligned} \qquad \begin{aligned} x + 3 &= 0 \\ x &= -3 \end{aligned} \qquad \begin{aligned} x - 3 &= 0 \\ x &= 3 \end{aligned}$$

Therefore, the solutions to this equation are $x = \{-3,-1,1,3\}$.

85. C: The line through the center of the box represents the median. The median test score for classes 1 and 2 is 82.

Note that for class 1, the median is a better representation of the data than the mean. There are two low outliers, points which lie outside of two standard deviations from the mean, which bring down the average test score. In cases such as this, the mean is not the best measure of central tendency.

86. D: 75% of the data in a set is above the first quartile. Since the first quartile for this set is 73, there is a 75% chance, or a probability of 0.75, that a student chosen at random from class 2 scored above a 73.

87. A: The range is the spread of the data. It can be calculated for each class by subtracting the lowest test score from the highest, or it can be determined visually from the graph. The difference between the highest and lowest test scores in class 1 is $98 - 23 = 75$ points. The range for each of the other classes is much smaller.

88. B: Get as many terms as possible out from the radical and any radicals out from the denominator:

$$\begin{aligned}\sqrt{\frac{-32x^4}{75y^5}} &= \sqrt{\frac{-16x^4 \cdot (2)}{25y^4 \cdot (3y)}} \\ &= \sqrt{\frac{-(4x^2)^2 \cdot (2)}{(5y^2)^2 \cdot (3y)}} \\ &= \frac{4x^2 i\sqrt{2}}{5y^2\sqrt{3y}} \cdot \frac{\sqrt{3y}}{\sqrt{3y}} \\ &= \frac{4x^2 i\sqrt{6y}}{15y^3}\end{aligned}$$

89. B: When the jeans are marked down by 30%, the cost is 70% of its original price. Thus, the reduced price of the dress can be written as $\frac{70}{100}x$, or $\frac{7}{10}x$, where x is the original price. When discounted an extra 15%, the jeans cost 85% of the reduced price, or $\frac{85}{100}\left(\frac{7}{10}x\right)$. This can be simplified to $\frac{17}{20}\left(\frac{7}{10}x\right)$. Multiply the fractions to get $\frac{119}{200}x$. So, the final price is $\frac{119}{200}$ of the original price.

90. C: A height of 5'11", or 71 inches, is one standard deviation above the mean. Since approximately 68% of the data is within one standard deviation of the mean, about 32% (100% − 68%) of the data is outside of one standard deviation within the mean. Normally distributed data is symmetric about the mean, which means that about 16% of the data lies below one standard deviation below the mean and about 16% of data lies above one standard deviation above the mean. Therefore, approximately 16% of individuals are 5'11" or taller, while approximately 84% of the population is shorter than 5'11". Multiply to find 84% of 200, $0.84 \times 200 = 168$. So, about 168 people from the selected group are shorter than 5'11".

91. A: Use the formula for the volume of a sphere to find the radius of the sphere:

$$\begin{aligned}V &= \frac{4}{3}\pi r^3 \\ 36\pi &= \frac{4}{3}\pi r^3 \\ 36 &= \frac{4}{3}r^3 \\ 27 &= r^3 \\ 3 &= r\end{aligned}$$

Then, substitute the point $(h, k, l) = (1, 0, -2)$ and the radius $r = 3$ into the equation of a sphere:

$$(x-h)^2 + (y-k)^2 + (z-l)^2 = r^2$$
$$(x-1)^2 + y^2 + (z+2)^2 = 3^2$$
$$(x-1)^2 + y^2 + (z+2)^2 = 9$$
$$x^2 - 2x + 1 + y^2 + z^2 + 4z + 4 = 9$$
$$x^2 + y^2 + z^2 - 2x + 4z = 4$$

92. A: Start by determining which values of x are not possible solutions. For this equation, x cannot equal –1 or –7 because these would result in denominator values of 0.

Then, solve the equation as normal.

$$\frac{x+2}{x+1} = \frac{x+9}{x+7} + \frac{2}{x+1}$$

$$\frac{x}{x+1} = \frac{x+9}{x+7}$$ Subtract $\frac{2}{x+1}$ from both sides of the equation.

$$(x)(x+7) = (x+9)(x+1)$$ Cross multiply to eliminate the fractions.

$$x^2 + 7x = x^2 + 10x + 9$$ Multiply the polynomials.

$$7x = 10x + 9$$ Subtract x^2 from both sides of the equation

$$-3x = 9$$ Subtract $10x$ from both sides of the equation.

$$x = -3$$ Divide both sides of the equation by –3.

Since –3 is not one of the values x cannot be equal to, our answer is $x = -3$.

93. B: A line graph is often used to show change over time. A Venn diagram shows the relationships among sets. A box-and-whisker plot displays how numeric data are distributed throughout the range. A pie chart shows the relationship of parts to a whole.

94. D: Step 6 established that $\angle BEA$ was a right angle. According to the definition of perpendicular lines, two lines that meet at a right angle are perpendicular.

95. D: In choice A, the teacher uses convenience sampling, which is a biased technique. A group of athletes is likely not representative of all high school girls. Choice B also represents convenience sampling, as all surveys were taken from the same neighborhood. While this likely included a variety of ages, career paths, etc., it most likely represented a narrow demographic since homes in a neighborhood tend to be similar in value. Choice C is biased because the participants are self-selected rather than randomly selected. It may be that people who have a strong opinion are more likely to respond than those who are more neutral, and this would give a skewed perspective of opinions. Choice D represents random selection since names are organized by computer generation rather than any particular demographic.

96. A: The student could use (3 × 75) ÷ 5 to solve this problem. Answer choice A could be expressed 3/5 × 75/1, which simplifies to (3 × 75)/5 = 225/5 = 45. The answer then is that 3/5 of 75 is 45.

97. B: The table shows a pattern that the number of wolves is multiplied by 1.5 each year.

Years after release	0	1	2	3	4
Number of wolves	16	24	36	54	81

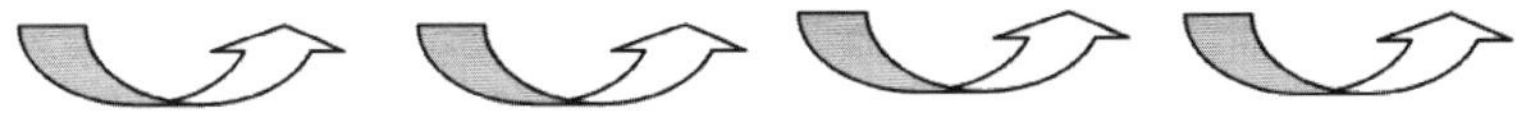

$\times 1.5$ $\times 1.5$ $\times 1.5$ $\times 1.5$

98. B: It is necessary to find the area of the floor by multiplying the dimensions together. However, since the dimensions are given in feet and we only know the price of carpeting per square yard, converting the dimensions from feet to yards first is helpful. Since there are 3 feet in a yard, dividing each of the dimensions by 3 will give us the measurements in yards.

$$18 \div 3 = 6$$
$$27 \div 3 = 9$$

So, the floor is 6 yards by 9 yards, which is an area of 54 square yards. Last, we multiply 54 by 14, since each square yard costs $14 and there are 54 square yards.

$$54 \times 14 = 756$$

So, the price of the carpet should be $756.

99. C: We can write the problem as a system of two linear equations. Let x be the number of gold coins and y be the number of silver coins. Since there are fifty coins total, we have $x + y = 50$ as one of the equations. If each gold coin weighs 12 ounces, then the total weight in ounces of the gold coins is $12x$. Similarly, the total weight in ounces of the silver coins is $8y$. Since all the coins together weigh 30 pounds, which is equal to $30 \times 16 = 480$ ounces, we have $12x + 8y = 480$. Because each term in this equation is divisible by 4, we can divide the whole equation by 4 to get $3x + 2y = 120$. This is not a required step, but does make the numbers a little smaller and more manageable.

We now have two equations: $x + y = 50$ and $3x + 2y = 120$. There are a number of ways to solve a system of equations like this. One is to the substitution method. We can solve the first equation for y to get $y = 50 - x$, and then substitute this into the second equation to get $3x + 2(50 - x) = 120$. After distributing the 2, we get $3x + 100 - 2x = 120$. Combining like terms gives $x + 100 = 120$. Finally, subtracting 100 from both sides yields $x = 20$. Thus, the number of gold coins is 20.

100. A: The net of a triangular prism has three rectangular faces and two triangular faces, and the rectangular faces must all be able to connect to each other directly. This is shown in choice A.